LET FREEDOM RING

The Words that Shaped our America

STERLING PUBLISHING CO., INC.

New York

Library of Congress Cataloging-in-Publication Data Available

Published by Sterling Publishing Company, Inc.
387 Park Avenue South, New York, NY 10016
Distributed in Canada by Sterling Publishing
Canadian Manda Group, One Atlantic Avenue, Suite 105
Toronto, Ontario, Canada M6K 3E7
Distributed in Great Britain and Europe by Cassell PLC
Wellington House, 125 Strand, London WC2R 0BB, England
Distributed in Australia by Capricorn Link (Australia) Pty Ltd.
P.O. Box 704, Windsor, NSW 2756, Australia
Printed in China
All rights reserved

Book design by Richard Oriolo

Sterling ISBN 0-8069-9287-5

Contents

I. Finding Freedom

II. Defining Freedom

III. Freedom Tested

IV. Carrying Freedom's Torch

V. Let Freedom Ring

FOREWORD

The words in this book define a nation. Most were written or spoken long before Americans of today were born; yet they continue to bind us, to each other and our past. This is as true for new immigrants as for Mayflower descendants. Nor is it simply familiarity with the words that explains our response. They resonate because they are imbued with significance from the historical events that produced them, because they evoke the meaning of those events like a poem evokes feeling, and because they capture the yearning of people everywhere. For example:

We hold these truths to be self-evident, that all men are created equal....

It is rather for us to be here dedicated to the great task remaining before us...that this nation, under God, shall have a new birth of freedom and that government of the people, by the people, for the people shall not perish from the earth.

Let every nation know, whether it wishes us well or ill, that we shall pay any price, bear any burden, meet any hardship, support any friend, oppose any foe, in order to assure the survival and the success of liberty.

I have a dream that one day on the red hills of Georgia the sons of former slaves and the sons of former slaveholders will be able to sit down together at the table of brotherhood.

President George W. Bush has now added to this heritage. Addressing Congress on September 20, 2001, nine days after terrorists crashed hijacked planes into the World Trade Center and the Pentagon, the President said this:

Tonight we are a country awakened to danger and called to defend freedom. Our grief has turned to anger and anger to resolution. Whether we bring our enemies to justice or justice to our enemies, justice will be done....
I will not forget this wound to our country or those who inflicted it. I will not yield; I will not rest; I will not relent in waging this struggle for freedom and security for the American people.

It is no coincidence that the President's words and the words contained in many of the documents in this book were written in times of conflict, turmoil, or war. It is in such times that a people are most in need of leadership, unity, and historical perspective. It is in such times that we seek affirmation of our national character and the values that inspire us. Some of the words printed here—from the Declaration of Independence and the Bill of Rights, to Lyndon Johnson's Great Society speech—commemorate our highest aspirations. Other words—in the speeches of Abraham Lincoln, Susan B. Anthony, and Martin Luther King, Jr.—remind us that we have often had to struggle to fulfill those aspirations.

We embrace equality, democracy, and fairness, but our actions have not always fostered these virtues. Yet we strive to do so. Our national journey is one of steady progress toward their fuller achievement. Of course, we are not and have never been unanimous in describing the aspirations we hold for our country or in our views of how to achieve them. Criticism of ourselves by ourselves is part of the heritage we hold dear.

Americans enjoy a level of liberty, security and prosperity unequaled in the history of the world and unsurpassed anywhere today. Our enjoyment of these blessings has become so routine a part of our lives that we often fail to recognize them. Freedom and safety are assumed, ordinary, and therefore unnoticed. But for billions of people who have lived and died on this earth, and billions alive today, the blessings we accept as ordinary are in fact extraordinary, even inconceivable.

The events of and after September 11 remind us that our blessings cannot be taken for granted. These events should inspire us to help others enjoy them and to realize that our own enjoyment likely depends on it. The words and pictures in this book offer a further lesson: Our liberty, security, and prosperity were achieved with struggle, vision, and sacrifice. Need for these qualities did not end with President Bush's speech to Congress. The need will never end.

STEPHEN GILLERS
Vice Dean and Professor of Law
New York University School of Law
New York, NY
November, 2001

PUBLISHER'S PREFACE

Almost 40 years ago, a very wise high school freshman-English teacher made the statement that, ". . . the words of our leaders are the foundations upon which our democracy has been built, and if we forget the words and their meaning, we can forget the democracy." That has stayed with me all these years, and this book is a tribute to that teacher and to America's freedom.

Events of recent times have focused our nation upon the values we have nurtured and protected for more than 225 years. Our country continues to stand at the forefront on issues of free speech, the rights of our citizens, and the equality of all who live here. We dedicate this book to those ideals, and to all the people of the United States.

Special notes of thanks are due to some very hardworking people. They made this 40-year-old dream, which they heard about just a few short weeks ago, into a reality. In the publishing world, a few weeks are a blink of an eye in the first stirrings of the life of a book. To bring an entire finished book to life in those few weeks is a publishing miracle.

Neither I, nor they, wrote the words in this book, of course, but they gathered together this superb collection, with outstanding photographs and illustrations, to represent the words that built and shaped our America. Thanks, Cassia Farkas, for hours and hours of work and dedication, bringing together a dream with far more completeness than I imagined possible. And thanks to Matt Silver, for uncovering, discovering, and sourcing out endless photographs and illustrations to make the words come alive even more; to Jeannine Ford and Richard Oriolo, who designed the book perfectly to respect and reflect the words; to Karen Nelson, who created the ideal jacket design to go with the title; and to Rick Willet, who produced this book far faster than it rightfully could have been done. I appreciate all of your dedication and talent.

And to my very special friend, Friday, thanks for your unwavering loyalty and the inspiration for this book and so many others. I'll miss you.

CHARLES NURNBERG

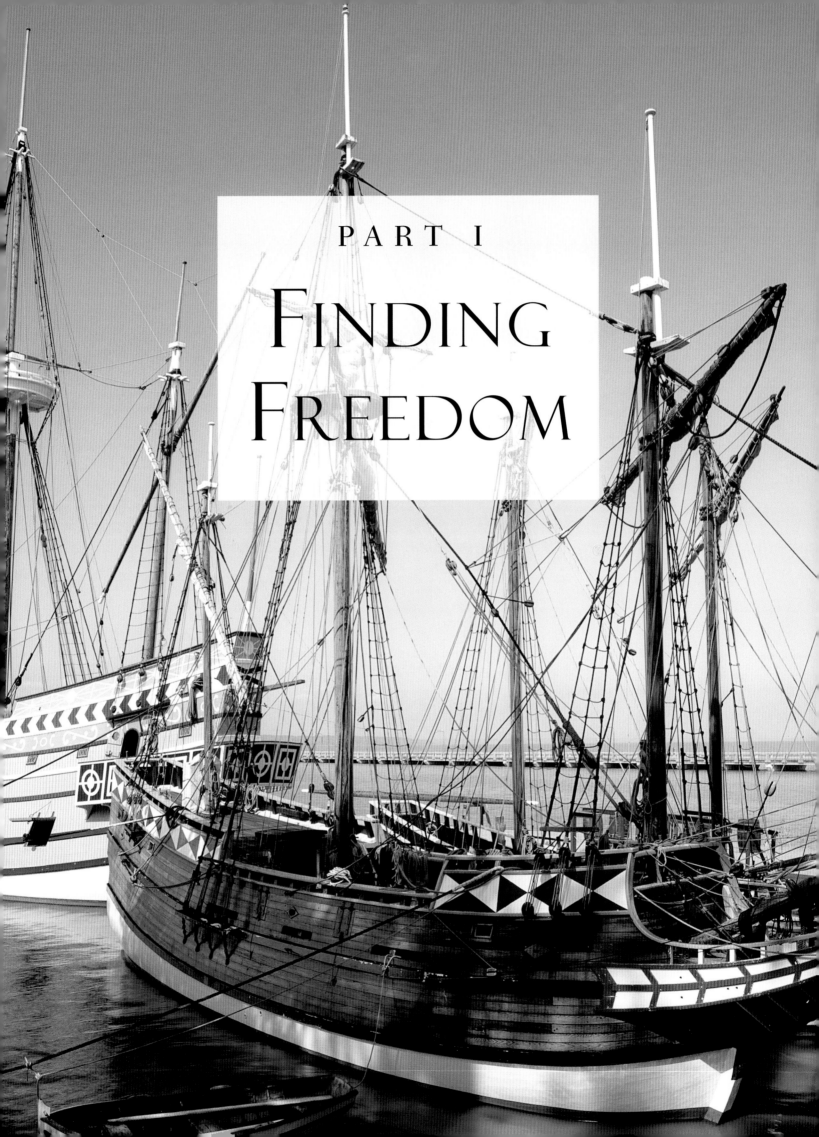

PART I
FINDING FREEDOM

Mayflower II, a model of the original Mayflower, in a living history reenactment.

THE MAYFLOWER COMPACT

1620

In the name of God, Amen. We, whose names are underwritten, the Loyal Subjects of our dread Sovereigne Lord, King James, by the Grace of God, of Great Britaine, France, and Ireland, King, Defender of the Faith, &c.

Having undertaken for the Glory of God, and Advancement of the Christian Faith, and the Honour of our King and Country, a Voyage to plant the first colony in the Northerne Parts of Virginia; doe, by these Presents, solemnly and mutually in the Presence of God and of one another, covenant and combine ourselves together into a civill Body Politick, for our better Ordering and Preservation, and Furtherance of the Ends aforesaid; And by Virtue hereof do enact, constitute, and frame, such just and equall Laws, Ordinances, Acts, Constitutions, and Offices, from time to time, as shall be thought most meete and convenient for the Generall Good of the Colonie; unto which we promise all due Submission and Obedience.

In Witness whereof we have hereunto subscribed our names at Cape Cod the eleventh of November, in the Raigne of our Sovereigne Lord, King James of England, France, and Ireland, the eighteenth, and of Scotland, the fiftie-fourth, Anno. Domini, 1620.

Mr. John Carver
Mr. Stephen Hopkins
Mr. William Bradford
Digery Priest
Mr. Edward Winslow
Thomas Williams
Mr. William Brewster
Gilbert Winslow
Isaac Allerton
Edmund Margesson
Miles Standish
Peter Brown
John Alden
Richard Bitteridge
John Turner
George Soule
Francis Eaton
Edward Tilly
James Chilton
John Tilly
John Craxton

Francis Cooke
John Billington
Thomas Rogers
Joses Fletcher
Thomas Tinker
John Goodman
John Ridgate
Mr. Samuel Fuller
Edward Fuller
Mr. Christopher Martin
Richard Clark
Mr. William Mullins
Richard Gardiner
Mr. William White
Mr. John Allerton
Mr. Richard Warren
Thomas English
John Howland
Edward Doten
Edward Liester

The Mayflower II anchored in Plymouth, Massachusetts. This reconstruction was made as a joint project between a British group called Project Mayflower and Plimouth Plantation. It was meticulously researched, constructed in England from authentic materials, then sailed across the Atlantic to Plymouth in the spring of 1957.

The Petition of Right

1628

The Petition exhibited to his Majesty by the Lords Spiritual and Temporal, and Commons, in this present Parliament assembled, concerning divers Rights and Liberties of the Subjects, with the King's Majesty's royal answer thereunto in full Parliament.

To the King's Most Excellent Majesty,

I Humbly show unto our Sovereign Lord the King, the Lords Spiritual and Temporal, and Commons in Parliament assembles, that whereas it is declared and enacted by a statute made in the time of the reign of King Edward I, commonly called Statutum de Tellagio non Concedendo, that no tallage or aid shall be laid or levied by the King or his heirs in this realm, without the good will and assent of the archbishops, bishops, earls, barons, knights, burgesses, and other the freemen of the commonalty of this realm; and by authority of parliament holden in the five-and-twentieth year of the reign of King Edward III, it is declared and enacted, that from thenceforth no person should be compelled to make any loans to the King against his will, because such loans were against reason and the franchise of the land; and by other laws of this realm it is provided, that none should be charged by any charge or imposition called a benevolence, nor by such like charge; by which statutes before mentioned, and other the good laws and statutes of this realm, your subjects have inherited this freedom, that they should not be compelled to contribute to any tax, tallage, aid, or other like charge not set by common consent, in Parliament.

II Yet nevertheless of late divers commissions directed to sundry commissioners in several counties, with instructions, have issued; by means whereof your people have been in divers places assembled, and required to lend certain sums of money unto your Majesty, and many of them, upon their refusal so to do, have had an oath administered unto them not warrantable by the laws or statutes of this realm, and have been constrained to become bound and make appearance and give utterance before your Privy Council and in other places, and others of them have been therefore imprisoned, confined, and sundry other ways molested and disquieted; and divers other charges have been laid and levied upon your people in several counties by lord lieutenants, deputy lieutenants, commissioners for musters, justices of peace and others, by command or direction from your Majesty, or your Privy Council, against the laws and free custom of the realm.

III And whereas also by the statute called <u>The Great Charter of the Liberties of England,</u> it is declared and enacted, that no freeman may be taken or imprisoned or be disseized of his freehold or liberties, or his free customs, or be outlawed or exiled, or in any manner destroyed, but by the lawful judgment of his peers, or by the law of the land.

IV And in the eight-and-twentieth year of the reign of King Edward III, it was declared and

Plymouth Rock today. Partly to commemorate it, but more importantly to protect it from souvenir hunters and the elements, Plymouth Rock is now enclosed by this monument.

enacted by authority of Parliament, that no man, of what estate or condition that he be, should be put out of his land or tenements, nor taken, nor imprisoned, nor disinherited nor put to death without being brought to answer by due process of law.

V Nevertheless, against the tenor of the said statutes, and other the good laws and statutes of your realm to that end provided, divers of your subjects have of late been imprisoned without any cause showed; and when for their deliverance they were brought before your justices by your Majesty's writs of habeas corpus, there to undergo and receive as the court should order, and their keepers commanded to certify the causes of their detainer, no cause was certified, but that they were detained by your Majesty's special command, signified by the lords of your Privy Council, and yet were returned back to several prisons, without being charged with anything to which they might make answer according to the law.

VI And whereas of late, great companies of soldiers and mariners have been dispersed into divers counties of the realm, and the inhabitants against their wills have been compelled to receive them into their houses, and there to suffer them to sojourn against the laws and customs of this realm, and to the great grievance and vexation of the people.

VII And whereas also by authority of Parliament, in the five-and-twentieth year of the reign of King Edward III, it is declared and enacted, that no man shall be forejudged of life or limb against the form of the Great Charter and the law of the land; and by the said Great Charter and the other laws and statutes of this your realm, no man ought to be adjudged to death but by the laws established in this your realm, either by the customs of the same realm, or by acts of Parliament: and whereas no offender of what kind soever is exempted from the proceedings to be used, and punishments to be inflicted by the laws and statutes of this your realm; nevertheless of late time divers commissions under your Majesty's great seal have issued forth, by which certain persons have been assigned and appointed commissioners with power and authority to proceed within the land, according to the justice of martial law, against such soldiers or mariners, or other dissolute persons joining with them, as should commit any murder, robbery, felony, mutiny, or other outrage or misdemeanor whatsoever, and by such summary course and order as is agreeable to martial law, and is used in armies in time of war, to proceed to the trial and condemnation of such offenders, and them to cause to be executed and put to death according to the law martial.

The sign for Concord, Massachusetts, one of the early settlements that would have been affected by the British injustices.

VIII By pretext whereof some of your Majesty's subjects have been by some of the said commissioners put to death, when and where, if by the laws and statutes of the land they had deserved death, by the same laws and statutes also they might, and by no other ought to have been judged and executed.

IX And also sundry grievous offenders, by color thereof claiming an exemption, have escaped the punishments due to them by the laws and statutes of this your realm, by reason that divers of your officers and ministers of justice have unjustly refused or forborne to proceed against such offenders according to the same laws and statutes, upon pretense that the said offenders were punishable only by martial law, and by authority of such commissions as aforesaid; which commissions, and all other of like nature, are wholly and directly contrary to the said laws and statutes of this your realm.

X They do therefore humbly pray your most excellent Majesty, that no man hereafter be compelled to make or yield any gift, loan, benevolence, tax, or such like charge, without common consent by act of Parliament; and that none be called to make answer, or take such oath, or to give attendance, or be confined, or otherwise molested or disquieted concerning the same or for refusal thereof; and that no freeman, in any such manner as is before mentioned, be imprisoned or detained; and that your Majesty would be pleased to remove the said soldiers and mariners, and that your people may not be so burdened in time to come; and that the aforesaid commissions, for proceeding by martial law, may be revoked and annulled; and that hereafter no commissions of like nature may issue forth to any person or persons whatsoever to

The House of the Seven Gables, built in 1668 in Salem, Massachusetts. Salem was first settled in 1626.

be executed as aforesaid, lest by color of them any of your Majesty's subjects be destroyed or put to death contrary to the laws and franchise of the land.

XI All which they most humbly pray of your most excellent Majesty as their rights and liberties, according to the laws and statutes of this realm; and that your Majesty would also vouchsafe to declare, that the awards, doings, and proceedings, to the prejudice of your people in any of the premises, shall not be drawn hereafter into consequence or example; and that your Majesty would be also graciously pleased, for the further comfort and safety of your people, to declare your royal will and pleasure, that in the things aforesaid all your officers and ministers shall serve you according to the laws and statutes of this realm, as they tender the honor of your Majesty, and the prosperity of this Kingdom.

THE MARYLAND TOLERATION ACT

1649

An Act Concerning Religion.

Forasmuch as in a well governed and Christian Common Wealth matters concerning Religion and the honor of God ought in the first place to bee taken, into serious consideracion and endeavoured to bee settled, Be it therefore ordered and enacted by the Right Honourable Cecilius Lord Baron of Baltemore absolute Lord and Proprietary of this Province with the advise and consent of this Generall Assembly:

That whatsoever person or persons within this Province and the Islands thereunto belonging shall from henceforth blaspheme God, that is Curse him, or deny our Saviour Jesus Christ to bee the sonne of God, or shall deny the holy Trinity the father sonne and holy Ghost, or the Godhead of any of the said Three persons of the Trinity or the Unity of the Godhead, or shall use or utter any reproachfull Speeches, words or language concerning the said Holy Trinity, or any of the said three persons thereof, shalbe punished with death and confiscation or forfeiture of all his or her lands and goods to the Lord Proprietary and his heires.

And bee it also Enacted by the Authority and with the advise and assent aforesaid, That whatsoever person or persons shall from henceforth use or utter any reproachfull words or Speeches concerning the blessed Virgin Mary the Mother of our Saviour or the holy Apostles or Evangelists or any of them shall in such case for the first offence forfeit to the said Lord Proprietary and his

On June 20, 1632, in the last weeks of his life, George Calvert, Lord Baltimore, a British catholic baron and early colonial entrepreneur, received from Charles I a colonial grant along with unprecedented powers. His heir, Cecil, inherited the 10-12 million acres of American land from his father and served as the designer and first Lord Proprietor of the colony that would become Maryland. From 1632–1675, Cecil skillfully preserved his charter rights from enemies. He established Maryland on a sound and prosperous footing (to the depletion of his personal fortune) and, being himself a catholic, consistently and innovatively promoted religious toleration for all Christians living in his colony.

heirs Lords and Proprietaries of this Province the summe of five pound Sterling or the value thereof to be Levyed on the goods and chattells of every such person soe offending, but in case such Offender or Offenders, shall not then have goods and chattells sufficient for the satisfyeing of such forfeiture, or that the same bee not otherwise speedily satisfyed that then such Offender or Offenders shalbe publiquely whipt and bee imprisoned during the pleasure of the Lord Proprietary or the Lieutenant or cheife Governor of this Province for the time being. And that every such Offender or Offenders for every second offence shall forfeit tenne pound sterling or the value thereof to bee levyed as aforesaid, or in case such offender or Offenders shall not then have goods and chattells within this Province sufficient for that purpose then to bee publiquely and severely whipt and imprisoned as before is expressed. And that every person or persons before mentioned offending herein the third time, shall for such third Offence forfeit all his lands and Goods and bee for ever banished and expelled out of this Province.

And be it also further Enacted by the same authority advise and assent that whatsoever person or persons shall from henceforth uppon any occasion of Offence or otherwise in a reproachful manner or Way declare call or denominate any person or persons whatsoever inhabiting, residing, traffiqueing, trading or comerceing within this Province or within any the Ports, Harbors, Creeks or Havens to the same belonging an heritick, Scismatick, Idolator, puritan, Independant, Prespiterian, popish prest, Jesuite, Jesuited papist, Lutheran, Calvenist, Anabaptist, Brownist, Antinomian, Barrowist, Roundhead, Separatist, or any other name or terme in a reproachfull manner relating to matter of Religion shall for every such Offence forfeit and loose the somme of tenne shillings sterling or

the value thereof to bee levyed on the goods and chattells of every such Offender and Offenders, the one half thereof to be forfeited and paid unto the person and persons of whom such reproachfull words are or shalbe spoken or uttered, and the other half thereof to the Lord Proprietary and his heires Lords and Proprietaries of this Province. But if such person or persons who shall at any time utter or speake any such reproachfull words or Language shall not have Goods or Chattells sufficient and overt within this Province to bee taken to satisfie the penalty aforesaid or that the same bee not otherwise speedily satisfyed, that then the person or persons soe offending shalbe publickly whipt, and shall suffer imprisonment without baile or maineprise [bail] untill hee, shee or they respectively shall satisfy the party soe offended or greived by such reproachfull Language by asking him or her respectively forgivenes publiquely for such his Offence before the Magistrate of cheife Officer or Officers of the Towne or place where such Offence shalbe given.

And be it further likewise Enacted by the Authority and consent aforesaid That every person and persons within this Province that shall at any time hereafter prophane the Sabbath or Lords day called Sunday by frequent swearing, drunkennes or by any uncivill or disorderly recreacion, or by working on that day when absolute necessity doth not require it shall for every such first offence forfeit 2s 6d sterling or the value thereof, and for the second offence 5s sterling or the value thereof, and for the third offence and soe for every time he shall offend in like manner afterwards 10s sterling or the value thereof. And in case such offender and offenders shall not have sufficient goods or chattells within this Province to satisfy any of the said Penalties respectively hereby imposed for prophaning the Sabbath or Lords day called Sunday as aforesaid, That in Every such case the partie soe offending shall for the first and second offence in that kinde be imprisoned till hee or shee shall publickly in open Court before the cheife Commander Judge or Magistrate, of that County Towne or precinct where such offence shalbe committed acknowledg the Scandall and offence he hath in that respect given against God and the good and civill Governement of this Province, And for the third offence and for every time after shall also bee publickly whipt.

And whereas the inforceing of the conscience in matters of Religion hath frequently fallen out to be of dangerous Consequence in those commonwealthes where it hath been practised, And for the more quiett and peaceable governement of this Province, and the better to preserve mutuall Love and amity amongst the Inhabitants thereof, Be it Therefore also by the Lord Proprietary with the advise and consent of this Assembly Ordeyned and enacted (except as in this present Act is before Declared and sett forth) that noe person or persons whatsoever within this Province, or the Islands, Ports, Harbors, Creekes, or havens thereunto belonging professing to beleive in Jesus Christ, shall from henceforth bee any waies troubled, Molested or discountenanced for or in respect of his or her religion nor in the free exercise thereof within this Province or the Islands thereunto belonging nor any way compelled to the beleife or exercise of any other Religion against his or her consent, soe as they be not unfaithfull to the Lord Proprietary, or molest or conspire against the civill Governement established or to bee established in this Province under him or his heires. And that all and every person and persons that shall presume Contrary to this Act and the true intent and meaning thereof directly or indirectly either in person or estate will-fully to wrong disturbe trouble or molest any person whatsoever within this Province professing to beleive in Jesus Christ for or in respect of his or her religion or the free exercise thereof within this Province other than is provided for in this Act that such person or persons soe offending, shalbe compelled to pay trebble damages to the party soe wronged or molested, and for every such offence shall also forfeit 20s sterling in money or the value thereof, half thereof for the use of the Lord Proprietary, and his heires Lords and Proprietaries of this Province, and the other half for the use of the party soe wronged or molested as aforesaid, Or if the partie soe offending as aforesaid shall refuse or bee unable to recompense the party soe wronged, or to satisfy such fyne or forfeiture, then such Offender shalbe severely punished by publick whipping and impris-onment during the pleasure of the Lord Proprietary, or his Lieutenant or cheife Governor of this Province for the tyme being without baile or maineprise.

And bee it further alsoe Enacted by the authority and consent aforesaid That the Sheriff or other Officer or Officers from time to time to bee appointed and authorized for that purpose, of the County Towne or precinct where every particular offence in this present Act conteyned shall happen at any time to bee committed and whereupon there is hereby a forfeiture fyne or

penalty imposed shall from time to time distraine and seise the goods and estate of every such person soe offending as aforesaid against this present Act or any part thereof, and sell the same or any part thereof for the full satisfaccion of such forfeiture, fine, or penalty as aforesaid, Restoring unto the partie soe offending the Remainder or overplus of the said goods or estate after such satisfaccion soe made as aforesaid.

The freemen have assented.

When Lord Baltimore founded his colony he could hardly have imagined Baltimore, Maryland would grow to look as it does here.

DECLARATION AND RESOLVES OF THE FIRST CONTINENTAL CONGRESS

October 1774

Whereas, since the close of the last war, the British Parliament, claiming a power of right to bind the people of America by statute in all cases whatsoever, hath, in some acts expressly imposed taxes on them, and in others, under various pretenses, but in fact for the purpose of raising a revenue, hath imposed rates and duties payable in these colonies, established a board of commissioners with unconstitutional powers, and extended the jurisdiction of courts of Admiralty not only for collecting the said duties, but for the trial of causes merely arising within the body of a county.

And whereas, in consequence of other statutes, judges who before held only estates at will in their offices, have been made dependent on the Crown alone for their salaries, and standing armies kept in times of peace. And it has lately been resolved in Parliament, that by force of a statute made in the thirty-fifth year of the reign of King Henry the Eighth, colonists may be transported to England, and tried there upon accusations for treasons and misprisions, or concealments of treasons committed in the colonies; and by a late statute, such trials have been directed in cases therein mentioned.

And whereas, in the last session of Parliament, three statutes were made; one entitled "An act to discontinue, in such manner and for such time as are therein mentioned, the landing and discharging, lading, or shipping of goods, wares and merchandise, at the town, and within the harbor of Boston in the province of Massachusetts-bay, in North America;" another, entitled "An act for the better regulating the government of the province of the Massachusetts-bay in New England;" and another, entitled "An act for the impartial administration of justice, in the cases of persons questioned for any act done by them in the execution of the law, or for the suppression of riots and tumults, in the province of the Massachusetts-bay, in New England."

And another statute was then made, "for making more effectual provision for the government of the province of Quebec," etc. All which statutes are impolitic, unjust, and cruel, as well as unconstitutional, and most dangerous and destructive of American rights.

And whereas, Assemblies have been frequently dissolved, contrary to the rights of the people, when they attempted to deliberate on grievances; and their dutiful, humble, loyal, & reasonable petitions to the crown for redress, have been repeatedly treated with contempt, by His Majesty's ministers of state:

A cartoon published by the writer, scientist and statesman Benjamin Franklin in the early 1770s, urging the colonies to unite and resist British rule

The good people of the several Colonies of New Hampshire, Massachusetts bay, Rhode Island and Providence plantations, Connecticut, New York, New Jersey, Pennsylvania, Newcastle Kent and Sussex on Delaware, Maryland, Virginia, North Carolina, and South Carolina, justly alarmed at these arbitrary proceedings of parliament and administration, have severally elected, constituted, and appointed deputies to meet, and sit in general Congress, in the city of Philadelphia, in order to obtain such establishment, as that their religion, laws, and liberties, may not be subverted:

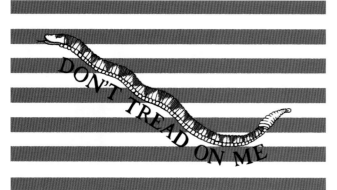

First Navy Jack of the Continental Navy. Patriots identified with the rattlesnake—a snake unique to America and deemed honorable because it gives fair warning before striking. The USS Kitty Hawk is the only ship authorized to fly this flag today.

Whereupon the deputies so appointed being now assembled, in a full and free representation of these Colonies, taking into their most serious consideration the best means of attaining the ends aforesaid, do in the first place, as Englishmen their ancestors in like cases have usually done, for asserting and vindicating their rights and liberties, declare,

That the inhabitants of the English Colonies in North America, by the immutable laws of nature, the principles of the English constitution, and the several charters or compacts, have the following Rights:

That our ancestors, who first settled these colonies, were at the time of their emigration from the mother country, entitled to all the rights, liberties, and immunities of free and natural born subjects within the realm of England.

That by such emigration they by no means forfeited, surrendered, or lost any of those rights, but that they were, and their descendants now are entitled to the exercise and enjoyment of all such of them, as their local and other circumstances enable them to exercise and enjoy.

That the foundation of English liberty, and of all free government, is a right in the people to participate in their legislative council: and as the English colonists are not represented, and from their local and other circumstances, cannot properly be represented in the British parliament, they are entitled to a free and exclusive power of legislation in their several provincial legislatures, where their right of representation can alone be preserved, in all cases of taxation and internal polity, subject only to the negative of their sovereign, in such manner as has been heretofore used and accustomed. But, from the necessity of the case, and a regard to the mutual interest of both countries, we cheerfully consent to the operation of such acts of the British parliament, as are bona fide restrained to the regulation of our external commerce, for the purpose of securing the commercial advantages of the whole empire to the mother country, and the commercial benefits of its respective members excluding every idea of taxation, internal or external, for raising a revenue on the subjects in America without their consent.

That the respective colonies are entitled to the common law of England, and more especially to the great and inestimable privilege of being tried by their peers of the vicinage, according to the course of that law.

That they are entitled to the benefit of such of the English statutes, as existed at the time of their colonization; and which they have, by experience, respectively found to be applicable to their several local and other circumstances.

That these, his majesty's colonies, are likewise entitled to all the immunities and privileges granted and confirmed to them by royal charters, or secured by their several codes of provincial laws.

The Flag of Vermont's Green Mountain Boys, founded and led by Ethan Allen. The group took Ft. Ticonderoga from the British in 1775, and helped to win the Battle of Bennington in 1777. Vermont became the 14th state in 1791.

That they have a right peaceably to assemble, consider of their grievances, and petition the King; and that all prosecutions, prohibitory proclamations, and commitments for the same, are illegal.

That the keeping a Standing army in these colonies, in times of peace, without the consent of the legislature of that colony in which such army is kept, is against law.

It is indispensably necessary to good government, and rendered essential by the English constitution, that the constituent branches of the legislature be independent of each other; that, therefore, the exercise of legislative power in several colonies, by a council appointed during pleasure, by the crown, is unconstitutional, dangerous, and destructive to the freedom of American legislation.

All and each of which the aforesaid deputies, in behalf of themselves, and their constituents, do claim, demand, and insist on, as their indubitable rights and liberties; which cannot be legally taken from them, altered or abridged by any power whatever, without their own consent, by their representatives in their several provincial legislatures.

In the course of our inquiry, we find many infringements and violations of the foregoing rights, which, from an ardent desire that harmony and mutual intercourse of affection and interest may be restored, we pass over for the present, and proceed to state such acts and measures as have been adopted since the last war, which demonstrate a system formed to enslave America.

DON'T TREAD ON ME

Resolved, That the following acts of Parliament are infringements and violations of the rights of the colonists; and that the repeal of them is essentially necessary, in order to restore harmony between Great Britain and the American colonies, viz.:

The Gadsden flag, used by Commodore Esek Hopkins, the first Commander in Chief of the new Continental Fleet, when his ships put to sea in February, 1776.

The several Acts of 4 Geo. 3, ch. 15 & ch. 34; 5 Geo. 3, ch. 25; 6 Geo. 3, ch. 52; 7 Geo. 3, ch. 41 & 46; 8 Geo. 3, ch. 22; which impose duties for the purpose of raising a revenue in America, extend the powers of the admiralty courts beyond their ancient limits, deprive the American subject of trial by jury, authorize the judges' certificate to indemnify the prosecutor from damages that he might otherwise be liable to, requiring oppressive security from a claimant of ships and goods seized before he shall be allowed to defend his property; and are subversive of American rights.

Also the 12 Geo. 3, ch. 24, entitled "An act for the better preserving his Majesty's dockyards, magazines, ships, ammunition, and stores," which declares a new offense in America, and deprives the American subject of a constitutional trial by jury of the vicinage, by authorizing the trial of any person charged with the committing any offense described in the said act, out of the realm, to be indicted and tried for the same in any shire or county within the realm.

Also the three acts passed in the last session of parliament, for stopping the port and blocking up the harbor of Boston, for altering the charter & government of the Massachusetts bay, and that which is entitled "An Act for the better administration of Justice," &c.

Also the act passed the same session for establishing the Roman Catholic Religion in the province of Quebec, abolishing the equitable system of English laws, and erecting a tyranny there, to the great danger, from so great a dissimilarity of Religion, law, and government, of the neighboring British colonies by the assistance of whose blood and treasure the said country was conquered from France.

Also the act passed the same session for the better providing suitable quarters for officers and soldiers in his Majesty's service in North America.

Also, that the keeping a standing army in several of these colonies, in time of peace, without the consent of the legislature of that colony in which the army is kept, is against law.

To these grievous acts and measures Americans cannot submit, but in hopes that their fellow subjects in Great Britain will, on a revision of them, restore us to that state in which both countries found happiness and prosperity, we have for the present only resolved to pursue the following peaceable measures: 1st. To enter into a non-importation, non-consumption, and non-exportation agreement or association. 2. To prepare an address to the people of Great Britain, and a memorial to the inhabitants of British America, & 3. To prepare a loyal address to his Majesty, agreeable to resolutions already entered into.

A view of Boston today. It is strange to imagine this cosmopolitan harbor as the site of the Boston Tea Party.

"GIVE ME LIBERTY OR GIVE ME DEATH"

Patrick Henry, March 23, 1775

No man thinks more highly than I do of the patriotism, as well as abilities, of the very worthy gentlemen who have just addressed the House. But different men often see the same subject in different lights; and, therefore, I hope it will not be thought disrespectful to those gentlemen if, entertaining as I do opinions of a character very opposite to theirs, I shall speak forth my sentiments freely and without reserve. This is no time for ceremony. The questing before the House is one of awful moment to this country. For my own part, I consider it as nothing less than a question of freedom or slavery; and in proportion to the magnitude of the subject ought to be the freedom of the debate. It is only in this way that we can hope to arrive at truth, and fulfill the great responsibility which we hold to God and our country. Should I keep back my opinions at such a time, through fear of giving offense, I should consider myself as guilty of treason towards my country, and of an act of disloyalty toward the Majesty of Heaven, which I revere above all earthly kings.

Mr. President, it is natural to man to indulge in the illusions of hope. We are apt to shut our eyes against a painful truth, and listen to the song of that siren till she transforms us into beasts. Is this the part of wise men, engaged in a great and arduous struggle for liberty? Are we disposed to be of the number of those who, having eyes, see not, and, having ears, hear not, the things which so nearly concern their temporal salvation? For my part, whatever anguish of spirit it may cost, I am willing to know the whole truth; to know the worst, and to provide for it.

I have but one lamp by which my feet are guided, and that is the lamp of experience. I know of no way of judging of the future but by the past. And judging by the past, I wish to know what there has been in the conduct of the British ministry for the last ten years to justify those hopes with which gentlemen have been pleased to solace themselves and the House. Is it that insidious smile with which our petition has been lately received? Trust it not, sir; it will prove a snare to your feet. Suffer not yourselves to be betrayed with a kiss. Ask yourselves how this gracious reception of our petition comports with those warlike preparations which cover our waters and darken our land. Are fleets and armies necessary to a work of love and reconciliation? Have we shown ourselves so unwilling to be reconciled that force must be called in to win back our love? Let us not deceive ourselves, sir. These are the implements of

American statesman and patriot Patrick Henry (1736–1799) addressing the Assembly in support of the American revolution in 1775.

war and subjugation; the last arguments to which kings resort. I ask gentlemen, sir, what means this martial array, if its purpose be not to force us to submission? Can gentlemen assign any other possible motive for it? Has Great Britain any enemy, in this quarter of the world, to call for all this accumulation of navies and armies? No, sir, she has none. They are meant for us: they can be meant for no other. They are sent over to bind and rivet upon us those chains which the British ministry have been so long forging. And what have we to oppose to them? Shall we try argument? Sir, we have been trying that for the last ten years. Have we anything new to offer upon the subject? Nothing. We have held the subject up in every light of which it is capable; but it has been all in vain. Shall we resort to entreaty and humble supplication? What terms shall we find which have not been already exhausted? Let us not, I beseech you, sir, deceive ourselves. Sir, we have done everything that could be done to avert the storm which is now coming on. We have petitioned; we have remonstrated; we have supplicated; we have prostrated ourselves before the throne, and have implored its interposition to arrest the tyrannical hands of the ministry and Parliament. Our petitions have been slighted; our remonstrances have produced additional violence and insult; our supplications have been disregarded; and we have been spurned, with contempt, from the foot of the throne! In vain, after these things, may we indulge the fond hope of peace and reconciliation. There is no longer any room for hope. If we wish to be free—if we mean to preserve inviolate those inestimable privileges for which we have been so long contending—if we mean not basely to abandon the noble struggle in which we have been so long engaged, and which we have pledged ourselves never to abandon until the glorious object of our contest shall be obtained—we must fight! I repeat it, sir, we must fight! An appeal to arms and to the God of hosts is all that is left us!

They tell us, sir, that we are weak; unable to cope with so formidable an adversary. But when shall we be stronger? Will it be the next week, or the next year? Will it be when we are totally disarmed, and when a British guard shall be stationed in every house? Shall we gather strength by irresolution and inaction? Shall we acquire the means of effectual resistance by lying supinely on our backs and hugging the delusive phantom of hope, until our enemies shall have bound us hand and foot? Sir, we are not weak if we make a proper use of those means which the God of nature hath placed in our power. The millions of people, armed in the holy cause of liberty, and in such a country as that which we possess, are invincible by any force which our enemy can send against us. Besides, sir, we shall not fight our battles alone. There is a just God who presides over the destinies of nations, and who will raise up friends to fight our battles for us. The battle, sir, is not to the strong alone; it is to the vigilant, the active, the brave. Besides, sir, we have no election. If we were base enough to desire it, it is now too late to retire from the contest. There is no retreat but in submission and slavery! Our chains are forged! Their clanking may be heard on the plains of Boston! The war is inevitable—and let it come! I repeat it, sir, let it come.

It is in vain, sir, to extenuate the matter. Gentlemen may cry, Peace, Peace—but there is no peace. The war is actually begun! The next gale that sweeps from the north will bring to our ears the clash of resounding arms! Our brethren are already in the field! Why stand we here idle? What is it that gentlemen wish? What would they have? Is life so dear, or peace so sweet, as to be purchased at the price of chains and slavery? Forbid it, Almighty God! I know not what course others may take; but as for me, give me liberty or give me death!

PAUL REVERE'S RIDE

By Henry Wadsworth Longfellow

Listen my children and you shall hear
Of the midnight ride of Paul Revere,
On the eighteenth of April, in Seventy-five;
Hardly a man is now alive
Who remembers that famous day and year.

He said to his friend, "If the British march
By land or sea from the town to-night,
Hang a lantern aloft in the belfry arch
Of the North Church tower as a signal
   light,—
One if by land, and two if by sea;
And I on the opposite shore will be,
Ready to ride and spread the alarm
Through every Middlesex village and farm,
For the country folk to be up and to arm."

Then he said "Good-night!" and with muffled
   oar
Silently rowed to the Charlestown shore,
Just as the moon rose over the bay,
Where swinging wide at her moorings lay
The Somerset, British man-of-war;
A phantom ship, with each mast and spar
Across the moon like a prison bar,
And a huge black hulk, that was magnified
By its own reflection in the tide.

Meanwhile, his friend through alley and street
Wanders and watches, with eager ears,
Till in the silence around him he hears
The muster of men at the barrack door,
The sound of arms, and the tramp of feet,
And the measured tread of the grenadiers,
Marching down to their boats on the shore.
Then he climbed the tower of the Old North
   Church,

By the wooden stairs, with stealthy tread,
To the belfry chamber overhead,
And startled the pigeons from their perch
On the sombre rafters, that round him made
Masses and moving shapes of shade,—
By the trembling ladder, steep and tall,
To the highest window in the wall,
Where he paused to listen and look down
A moment on the roofs of the town
And the moonlight flowing over all.

Beneath, in the churchyard, lay the dead,
In their night encampment on the hill,
Wrapped in silence so deep and still
That he could hear, like a sentinel's tread,
The watchful night-wind, as it went
Creeping along from tent to tent,
And seeming to whisper, "All is well!"
A moment only he feels the spell
Of the place and the hour, and the secret
   dread
Of the lonely belfry and the dead;
For suddenly all his thoughts are bent
On a shadowy something far away,
Where the river widens to meet the bay,—
A line of black that bends and floats
On the rising tide like a bridge of boats.

Meanwhile, impatient to mount and ride,
Booted and spurred, with a heavy stride
On the opposite shore walked Paul Revere.
Now he patted his horse's side,
Now he gazed at the landscape far and near,
Then, impetuous, stamped the earth,
And turned and tightened his saddle girth;
But mostly he watched with eager search
The belfry tower of the Old North Church,

The Paul Revere statue is located on the Prado in front of Boston's famous Old North Church (built in 1723). The lanterns used to signal Paul Revere on his midnight ride were hung in the Church's Steeple. These historic sites, along with 16 others are part of The Freedom Trail, a two mile walking tour through Boston.

As it rose above the graves on the hill,
Lonely and spectral and sombre and still.
And lo! as he looks, on the belfry's height
A glimmer, and then a gleam of light!
He springs to the saddle, the bridle he turns,
But lingers and gazes, till full on his sight
A second lamp in the belfry burns.

A hurry of hoofs in a village street,
A shape in the moonlight, a bulk in the dark,
And beneath, from the pebbles, in passing, a
    spark
Struck out by a steed flying fearless and fleet;
That was all! And yet, through the gloom and the
    light,
The fate of a nation was riding that night;
And the spark struck out by that steed, in his
    flight,
Kindled the land into flame with its heat.
He has left the village and mounted the steep,
And beneath him, tranquil and broad and deep,
Is the Mystic, meeting the ocean tides;
And under the alders that skirt its edge,
Now soft on the sand, now loud on the ledge,
Is heard the tramp of his steed as he rides.

It was twelve by the village clock
When he crossed the bridge into Medford town.
He heard the crowing of the cock,
And the barking of the farmer's dog,
And felt the damp of the river fog,
That rises after the sun goes down.

It was one by the village clock,
When he galloped into Lexington.
He saw the gilded weathercock
Swim in the moonlight as he passed,

And the meeting-house windows, black and bare,
Gaze at him with a spectral glare,
As if they already stood aghast
At the bloody work they would look upon.

It was two by the village clock,
When he came to the bridge in Concord town.
He heard the bleating of the flock,
And the twitter of birds among the trees,
And felt the breath of the morning breeze
Blowing over the meadow brown.
And one was safe and asleep in his bed
Who at the bridge would be first to fall,
Who that day would be lying dead,
Pierced by a British musket ball.

You know the rest. In the books you have read
How the British Regulars fired and fled,—
How the farmers gave them ball for ball,
From behind each fence and farmyard wall,
Chasing the redcoats down the lane,
Then crossing the fields to emerge again
Under the trees at the turn of the road,
And only pausing to fire and load.

So through the night rode Paul Revere;
And so through the night went his cry of alarm
To every Middlesex village and farm,—
A cry of defiance, and not of fear,
A voice in the darkness, a knock at the door,
And a word that shall echo for evermore!
For, borne on the night-wind of the Past,
Through all our history, to the last,
In the hour of darkness and peril and need,
The people will waken and listen to hear
The hurrying hoof-beats of that steed,
And the midnight message of Paul Revere.

Letter to Martha from George Washington

1775

It has been determined in Congress, that the whole army raised for the defence of the American cause shall be put under my care, and that it is necessary for me to proceed immediately to Boston to take upon me the command of it.

You may believe me, my dear Patsy, when I assure you in the most solemn manner that, so far from seeking this appointment, I have used every endeavor in my power to avoid it, not only from my unwillingness to part with you and the family, but from a consciousness of its being a trust too great for my capacity, and that I should enjoy more real happiness in one month with you at home than I have the most distant prospect of finding abroad . . . .

It was utterly out of my power to refuse this appointment, without exposing my character to such censure as would have reflected dishonor upon myself, and have given pain to my friends . . . .

I shall rely, therefore, confidently on that Providence which has heretofore preserved and been bountiful to me, not doubting but that I shall return safe to you in the fall.

Martha Custis was a young widow with two children when George Washington married her in January, 1759. At the time George wrote this letter to Martha, it was less than a year since her daughter had died of an epileptic seizure at age 17. Martha joined George for Christmas of 1775, remaining with him in Massachusetts until June of 1776, when she returned to their home in Virginia. The war would keep them from seeing each other again until March of 1777. Before her death in 1799, Martha burned all but two letters exchanged between George and herself.

THE DECLARATION
OF INDEPENDENCE

In Congress, July 4, 1776

The unanimous Declaration of the thirteen United States of America.

When in the Course of human events, it becomes necessary for one people to dissolve the political bands which have connected them with another, and to assume among the powers of the earth, the separate and equal station to which the Laws of Nature and of Nature's God entitle them, a decent respect to the opinions of mankind requires that they should declare the causes which impel them to the separation.

We hold these truths to be self-evident, that all men are created equal, that they are endowed by their Creator with certain unalienable Rights, that among these are Life, Liberty, and the pursuit of Happiness. That to secure these rights, Governments are instituted among Men, deriving their just powers from the consent of the governed. That whenever any Form of Government becomes destructive of these ends, it is the Right of the People to alter or to abolish it, and to institute new Government, laying its foundation on such principles and organizing its powers in such form, as to them shall seem most likely to effect their Safety and Happiness.

Prudence, indeed, will dictate that Governments long established should not be changed for light and transient causes; and accordingly all experience hath shewn, that mankind are more disposed to suffer, while evils are sufferable, than to right themselves by abolishing the forms to which they are accustomed.

But when a long train of abuses and usurpations, pursuing invariably the same object evinces a design to reduce them under absolute Despotism, it is their right, it is their duty, to throw off such Government, and to provide new Guards for their future security.

A Currier & Ives print depicting the committee that drafted the Declaration of Independence. From left: Thomas Jefferson (1743–1826), Roger Sherman (1721–1793), Benjamin Franklin (1706–1790), Robert R. Livingston (1746–1813) and John Adams (1735–1826).

4th of July, 1776—the final version of the American Declaration of Independence.

Such has been the patient sufferance of these Colonies; and such is now the necessity which constrains them to alter their former Systems of Government. The history of the present King of Great Britain [George III] is a history of repeated injuries and usurpations, all having in direct object the establishment of an absolute Tyranny over these States. To prove this, let Facts be submitted to a candid world.

He has refused his Assent to Laws, the most wholesome and necessary for the public good.

He has forbidden his Governors to pass Laws of immediate and pressing importance, unless suspended in their operation till his Assent should be obtained, and when so suspended, he has utterly neglected to attend to them.

He has refused to pass other Laws for the accommodation of large districts of people, unless those people would relinquish the right of Representation in the Legislature, a right inestimable to them and formidable to tyrants only.

He has called together legislative bodies at places unusual, uncomfortable, and distant from the depository of their public Records, for the sole purpose of fatiguing them into compliance with his measures.

He has dissolved Representative Houses repeatedly, for opposing with manly firmness his invasions on the rights of the people.

He has refused for a long time, after such dissolutions, to cause others to be elected; whereby the Legislative powers, incapable of Annihilation, have returned to the People at large for their exercise; the State remaining in the meantime exposed to all the dangers of invasion from without, and convulsions within.

He has endeavoured to prevent the population of these States; for that purpose obstructing the Laws for Naturalization of Foreigners; refusing to pass others to encourage their migrations hither, and raising the conditions of new Appropriations of Lands.

He has obstructed the Administration of Justice, by refusing his Assent to Laws for establishing Judiciary powers.

He has made Judges dependent on his Will alone, for the tenure of their offices, and the amount and payment of their salaries.

He has erected a multitude of New Offices, and sent hither swarms of Officers to harass our people, and eat out their substance.

He has kept among us, in times of peace, Standing Armies, without the consent of our legislatures.

He has affected to render the Military independent of and superior to the Civil power.

He has combined with others to subject us to a jurisdiction foreign to our constitution and unacknowledged by our laws; giving his Assent to their Acts of pretended Legislation:

- For quartering large bodies of armed troops among us:

- For protecting them by a mock Trial from punishment for any Murders which they should commit on the Inhabitants of these States:

- For cutting off our Trade with all parts of the world:

- For imposing Taxes on us without our Consent:

- For depriving us in many cases of the benefits of Trial by Jury:

- For transporting us beyond Seas to be tried for pretended offences:

- For abolishing the free System of English Laws in a neighbouring Province, establishing therein an Arbitrary government, and enlarging its Boundaries so as to render it at once an example and fit instrument for introducing the same absolute rule into these Colonies:

- For taking away our Charters, abolishing our most valuable Laws and altering fundamentally the Forms of our Governments:

- For suspending our own Legislatures, and declaring themselves invested with power to legislate for us in all cases whatsoever.

He has abdicated Government here by declaring us out of his Protection and waging War against us.

He has plundered our seas, ravaged our Coasts, burnt our towns, and destroyed the lives of our people.

He is at this time transporting large Armies of foreign Mercenaries to complete the works of death, desolation and tyranny, already begun with circumstances of cruelty and perfidy scarcely paralleled in the most barbarous ages, and totally unworthy the Head of a civilized nation.

He has constrained our fellow Citizens taken Captive on the high Seas to bear Arms against their Country, to become the executioners of their friends and Brethren, or to fall themselves by their Hands.

He has excited domestic insurrections amongst us, and has endeavoured to bring on the inhabitants of our frontiers, the merciless Indian Savages, whose known rule of warfare is an undistinguished destruction of all ages, sexes and conditions.

In every stage of these Oppressions We have Petitioned for Redress in the most humble terms. Our repeated Petitions have been answered only by repeated injury. A Prince, whose character is thus marked by every act which may define a Tyrant, is unfit to be the ruler of a free people.

Nor have We been wanting in attentions to our British brethren.

- We have warned them from time to time of attempts by their legislature to extend an unwarrantable jurisdiction over us.

- We have reminded them of the circumstances of our emigration and settlement here.

- We have appealed to their native justice and magnanimity, and we have conjured them by the ties of our common kindred to disavow these usurpations, which would inevitably interrupt our connections and correspondence.

They too have been deaf to the voice of justice and of consanguinity. We must, therefore, acquiesce in the necessity, which denounces our Separation, and hold them, as we hold the rest of mankind, Enemies in War, in Peace Friends.

We, therefore, the Representatives of the United States of America, in General Congress, Assembled, appealing to the Supreme Judge of the world for the rectitude of our intentions, do, in the Name, and by the authority of the good People of these Colonies, solemnly publish and declare,

That these United Colonies are, and of Right ought to be Free and Independent States; that they are Absolved from all Allegiance to the British Crown, and that all political connection between them and the State of Great Britain is and ought to be totally dissolved;

and that as Free and Independent States, they have full Power to levy War, conclude Peace, contract Alliances, establish Commerce,

and to do all other Acts and Things which Independent States may of right do.

And for the support of this Declaration, with a firm reliance on the protection of Divine Providence, we mutually pledge to each other our Lives, our Fortunes, and our sacred Honor.

The signers of the Declaration represented the new states as follows:

Birth of Our Nation's Flag.

Betsy Ross unfolds the first American flag for General George Washington and members of Congress. The flag is reputed to have been commissioned and made in her home at 239 Arch Street in Philadelphia.

New Hampshire: Josiah Bartlett, William Whipple, Matthew Thornton

Massachusetts: John Hancock, Samual Adams, John Adams, Robert Treat Paine, Elbridge Gerry

Rhode Island: Stephen Hopkins, William Ellery

Connecticut: Roger Sherman, Samuel Huntington, William Williams, Oliver Wolcott

New York: William Floyd, Philip Livingston, Francis Lewis, Lewis Morris

New Jersey: Richard Stockton, John Witherspoon, Francis Hopkinson, John Hart, Abraham Clark

Pennsylvania: Robert Morris, Benjamin Rush, Benjamin Franklin, John Morton, George Clymer, James Smith, George Taylor, James Wilson, George Ross

Delaware: Caesar Rodney, George Read, Thomas McKean

Maryland: Samuel Chase, William Paca, Thomas Stone, Charles Carroll of Carrollton

Virginia: George Wythe, Richard Henry Lee, Thomas Jefferson, Benjamin Harrison, Thomas Nelson, Jr., Francis Lightfoot Lee, Carter Braxton

North Carolina: William Hooper, Joseph Hewes, John Penn

South Carolina: Edward Rutledge, Thomas Heyward, Jr., Thomas Lynch, Jr., Arthur Middleton

Georgia: Button Gwinnett, Lyman Hall, George Walton

"I Regret I Have but One Life to Give"

Nathan Hale, September 22, 1776

American Revolutionary soldier Nathan Hale (1755–1776) receives his instructions from General Washington. A Connecticut native, he volunteered to cross Long Island Sound and penetrate the British lines on Long Island disguised as a schoolteacher in order to gather intelligence for Washington. Waiting to return, he emerged too soon from cover when he caught sight of a boat. It turned out to be a British patrol. They found his notes concealed in the sole of his shoe and took him to New York City, where he was hanged as a spy.

British soldiers preparing to hang the American patriot and spy, Nathan Hale. Before his execution, when asked if he had any last words, Hale declared, "I regret I have but one life to give for my country."

"THESE ARE THE TIMES THAT TRY MEN'S SOULS"

Thomas Paine, December 23, 1776

These are the times that try men's souls. The summer soldier and the sunshine patriot will, in this crisis, shrink from the service of their country; but he that stands it now, deserves the love and thanks of man and woman. Tyranny, like hell, is not easily conquered; yet we have this consolation with us, that the harder the conflict, the more glorious the triumph. What we obtain too cheap, we esteem too lightly: it is dearness only that gives every thing its value. Heaven knows how to put a proper price upon its goods; and it would be strange indeed if so celestial an article as freedom should not be highly rated. Britain, with an army to enforce her tyranny, has declared that she has a right (not only to tax) but "to bind us in all cases whatsoever," and if being bound in that manner, is not slavery, then is there not such a thing as slavery upon earth. Even the expression is impious; for so unlimited a power can belong only to God.

Whether the independence of the continent was declared too soon, or delayed too long, I will not now enter into as an argument; my own simple opinion is, that had it been eight months earlier, it would have been much better. We did not make a proper use of last winter, neither could we, while we were in a dependent state. However, the fault, if it were one, was all our own;* we have none to blame but ourselves. But no great deal is lost yet. All that Howe has been doing for this month past, is rather a ravage than a conquest, which the spirit of the Jerseys, a year ago, would have quickly repulsed, and which time and a little resolution will soon recover.

I have as little superstition in me as any man living, but my secret opinion has ever been, and still is, that God Almighty will not give up a people to military destruction, or leave them unsupportedly to perish, who have so earnestly and so repeatedly sought to avoid the calamities of war, by every decent method which wisdom could invent. Neither have I so much of the infidel in me, as to suppose that He has relinquished the government of the world, and given us up to the care of devils; and as I do not, I cannot see on what grounds the king of Britain can look up to heaven for help against us: a common murderer, a highwayman, or a house-breaker, has as good a pretence as he.

American Revolutionary philosopher Thomas Paine (1737–1809). He published this article under the title "The American Crisis" in the pamphlet, **Common Sense.**

Living History enactment of a Revolutionary War scene.

'Tis surprising to see how rapidly a panic will sometimes run through a country. All nations and ages have been subject to them. Britain has trembled like an ague at the report of a French fleet of flat-bottomed boats; and in the fourteenth [fifteenth] century the whole English army, after ravaging the kingdom of France, was driven back like men petrified with fear; and this brave exploit was performed by a few broken forces collected and headed by a woman, Joan of Arc. Would that heaven might inspire some Jersey maid to spirit up her countrymen, and save her fair fellow sufferers from ravage and ravishment! Yet panics, in some cases, have their uses; they produce as much good as hurt. Their duration is always short; the mind soon grows through them, and acquires a firmer habit than before. But their peculiar advantage is, that they are the touchstones of sincerity and hypocrisy, and bring things and men to light, which might otherwise have lain forever undiscovered. In fact, they have the same effect on secret traitors, which an imaginary apparition would have upon a private murderer. They sift out the hidden thoughts of man, and hold them up in public to the world. Many a disguised Tory has lately shown his head, that shall penitentially solemnize with curses the day on which Howe arrived upon the Delaware.

As I was with the troops at Fort Lee, and marched with them to the edge of Pennsylvania, I am well acquainted with many circumstances, which those who live at a distance know but little or nothing of. Our situation there was exceedingly cramped, the place being a narrow neck of land between the North River and the Hackensack. Our force was inconsiderable, being not one-fourth so great as Howe could bring against us. We had no army at hand to have relieved the garrison, had we shut ourselves up and stood on our defence. Our ammunition, light artillery, and the best part of our stores, had been removed, on the apprehension that Howe would endeavor to penetrate the Jerseys, in which case Fort Lee could be of no use to us; for it must occur to every thinking man, whether in the army or not, that these kind of field forts are only for temporary purposes, and last in use no longer than the enemy directs his force against the particular object which such forts are raised to defend. Such was our situation and condition at Fort Lee on the morning of the 20th of November, when an officer arrived with information that the enemy with 200 boats had landed about seven miles above; Major General [Nathaniel] Green, who commanded the garrison, immediately ordered them under arms, and sent express to General Washington at the town of Hackensack, distant by the way of the ferry = six miles. Our first object was to secure the bridge over the Hackensack, which laid up the river between the enemy and us, about six miles from us, and three from them. General Washington arrived in about three-quarters of an hour, and marched at the head of the troops towards the bridge, which place I expected we should have a brush for; however, they did not choose to dispute it with us, and the greatest part of our troops went over the bridge, the rest over the ferry, except some which passed at a mill on a small creek, between the bridge and the ferry, and made their way through some marshy grounds up to the town of Hackensack, and there passed the river. We brought off as much baggage as the wagons could contain, the rest was lost. The simple object was to bring off the garrison, and march them on till they could be strengthened by the Jersey or Pennsylvania militia, so as to be enabled to make a stand. We staid four days at Newark, collected our out-posts with some of the Jersey militia, and marched out twice to meet the enemy, on being informed that they were advancing, though our numbers were greatly inferior to theirs. Howe, in my little opinion, committed a great error in generalship in not throwing a body of forces off from Staten Island through Amboy, by which means he might have seized all our stores at Brunswick, and intercepted our march into Pennsylvania; but if we believe the power of hell to be limited, we must likewise believe that their agents are under some providential control.

I shall not now attempt to give all the particulars of our retreat to the Delaware; suffice it for the present to say, that both officers and men, though greatly harassed and fatigued, frequently without rest, covering, or provision, the inevitable consequences of a long retreat, bore it with a manly and martial spirit. All their wishes centred in one, which was, that the country would turn out and help them to drive the enemy back. Voltaire has remarked that King William never appeared to full advantage but in difficulties and in action; the same remark may be made on General Washington, for the character fits him. There is a natural firmness in some minds which cannot be unlocked by trifles, but which, when unlocked, discovers a cabinet of fortitude; and I reckon it among those kind of public blessings, which we do not immediately see, that God hath blessed him with uninterrupted health, and given him a mind that can even flourish upon care.

George Washington urging on his threadbare troops at Princeton, on January 3, 1777.
His arrival turned the battle against the British.

I shall conclude this paper with some miscellaneous remarks on the state of our affairs; and shall begin with asking the following question, Why is it that the enemy have left the New England provinces, and made these middle ones the seat of war? The answer is easy: New England is not infested with Tories, and we are. I have been tender in raising the cry against these men, and used numberless arguments to show them their danger, but it will not do to sacrifice a world either to their folly or their baseness. The period is now arrived, in which either they or we must change our sentiments, or one or both must fall. And what is a Tory? Good God! what is he? I should not be afraid to go with a hundred Whigs against a thousand Tories, were they to attempt to get into arms. Every Tory is a coward; for servile, slavish, self-interested fear is the foundation of Toryism; and a man under such influence, though he may be cruel, never can be brave.

But, before the line of irrecoverable separation be drawn between us, let us reason the matter together: Your conduct is an invitation to the enemy, yet not one in a thousand of you has heart enough to join him. Howe is as much deceived by you as the American cause is injured by you. He expects you will all take up arms, and flock to his standard, with muskets on your shoulders. Your opinions are of no use to him, unless you support him personally, for 'tis soldiers, and not Tories, that he wants.

I once felt all that kind of anger, which a man ought to feel, against the mean principles that are held by the Tories: a noted one, who kept a tavern at Amboy, was standing at his door, with as pretty a child in his hand, about eight or nine years old, as I ever saw, and after speaking his mind as freely as he thought was prudent, finished with this unfatherly expression, "Well! give me peace in my day." Not a man lives on the continent but fully believes that a separation must some time or other finally take place, and a generous parent should have said, "If there must be trouble, let it be in my day, that my child may have peace;" and this single reflection, well applied, is sufficient to awaken every man to duty. Not a place upon earth might be so happy as America. Her situation is remote from all the wrangling world, and she has nothing to do but to trade with them. A man can distinguish himself between temper and principle, and I am as confident, as I am that God governs the world, that America will never be happy till she gets clear of foreign dominion. Wars, without ceasing, will break out till that period arrives, and the continent must in the end be conqueror; for though the flame of liberty may sometimes cease to shine, the coal can never expire.

America did not, nor does not want force; but she wanted a proper application of that force. Wisdom is not the purchase of a day, and it is no wonder that we should err at the first setting off. From an excess of tenderness, we were unwilling to raise an army, and trusted our cause to the temporary defence of a well-meaning militia. A summer's experience has now taught us better; yet with those troops, while they were collected, we were able to set bounds to the progress of the enemy, and, thank God! they are again assembling. I always considered militia as the best troops in the world for a sudden exertion, but they will not do for a long campaign. Howe, it is probable, will make an attempt on this city [Philadelphia]; should he fail on this side the Delaware, he is ruined. If he succeeds, our cause is not ruined. He stakes all on his side against a part on ours; admitting he succeeds, the consequence will be, that armies from both ends of the continent will march to assist their suffering friends in the middle states; for he cannot go everywhere, it is impossible. I consider Howe as the greatest enemy the Tories have; he is bringing a war into their country, which, had it not been for him and partly for themselves, they had been clear of. Should he now be expelled, I wish with all the devotion of a Christian, that the names of Whig and Tory may never more be mentioned; but should the Tories give him encouragement to come, or assistance if he come, I as sincerely wish that our next year's arms may expel them from the continent, and the Congress appropriate their possessions to the relief of those who have suffered in well-doing. A single successful battle next year will settle the whole. America could carry on a two years' war by the confiscation of the property of disaffected persons, and be made happy by their expulsion. Say not that this is revenge, call it rather the soft resentment of a suffering people, who, having no object in view but the good of all, have staked their own all upon a seemingly doubtful event. Yet it is folly to argue against determined hardness; eloquence may strike the ear, and the language of sorrow draw forth the tear of compassion, but nothing can reach the heart that is steeled with prejudice.

Quitting this class of men, I turn with the warm ardor of a friend to those who have nobly stood, and are yet determined to stand the matter out: I call not upon a few, but upon all: not on this state or that state, but on every state: up and help us; lay your shoulders to the wheel; better have too much force than too little, when so great an object is at stake. Let it be told to the future world, that in the depth of winter, when nothing but hope and virtue could survive, that the city and the country, alarmed at one common danger, came forth to meet and to repulse it. Say not that thousands are gone, turn out your tens of thousands; throw not the burden of the day upon Providence, but "show your faith by your works," that God may bless you. It matters not where you live, or what rank of life you hold, the evil or the blessing will reach you all. The far and the near, the home counties and the back, the rich and the poor, will suffer or rejoice alike. The heart that feels not now is dead; the blood of his children will curse his cowardice, who shrinks back at a time when a little might have saved the whole, and made them happy. I love the man that can smile in trouble, that can gather strength from distress, and grow brave by reflection. 'Tis the business of little minds to shrink; but he whose heart is firm, and whose conscience approves his conduct, will pursue his principles unto death. My own line of reasoning is to myself as straight and clear as a ray of light. Not all the treasures of the world, so far as I believe, could have induced me to support an offensive war, for I think it murder; but if a thief breaks into my house, burns and destroys my property, and kills or threatens to kill me, or those that are in it, and to "bind me in all cases whatsoever" to his absolute will, am I to suffer it? What signifies it to me, whether he who does it is a king or a common man; my countryman or not my countryman; whether it be done by an individual villain, or an army of them? If we reason to the root of things we shall find no difference; neither can any just cause be assigned why we should punish in the one case and pardon in the other. Let them call me rebel and welcome, I feel no concern from it; but I should suffer the misery of devils, were I to make a whore of my soul by swearing allegiance to one whose character is that of a sottish, stupid, stubborn, worthless, brutish man. I conceive likewise a horrid idea in receiving mercy from a being, who at the last day shall be shrieking to the rocks and mountains to cover him, and fleeing with terror from the orphan, the widow, and the slain of America.

There are cases which cannot be overdone by language, and this is one. There are persons, too, who see not the full extent of the evil which threatens them; they solace themselves with hopes that the enemy, if he succeed, will be merciful. It is the madness of folly, to expect mercy from those who have refused to do justice; and even mercy, where conquest is the object, is only a trick of war; the cunning of the fox is as murderous as the violence of the wolf, and we ought to guard equally against both. Howe's first object is, partly by threats and partly by promises, to terrify or seduce the people to deliver up their arms and receive mercy. The ministry recommended the same plan to Gage, and this is what the Tories call making their peace, "a peace which passeth all understanding" indeed! A peace which would be the immediate forerunner of a worse ruin than any we have yet thought of. Ye men of Pennsylvania, do reason upon these things! Were the back counties to give up their arms, they would fall an easy prey to the Indians, who are all armed: this perhaps is what some Tories would not be sorry for. Were the home counties to deliver up their arms, they would be exposed to the resentment of the back counties who would then have it in their power to chastise their defection at pleasure. And were any one state to give up its arms, that state must be garrisoned by all Howe's army of Britons and Hessians to preserve it from the anger of the rest. Mutual fear is the principal link in the chain of mutual love, and woe be to that state that breaks the compact. Howe is mercifully inviting you to barbarous destruction, and men must be either rogues or fools that will not see it. I dwell not upon the vapors of imagination; I bring reason to your ears, and, in language as plain as A, B, C, hold up truth to your eyes.

I thank God, that I fear not. I see no real cause for fear. I know our situation well, and can see the way out of it. While our army was collected, Howe dared not risk a battle; and it is no credit to him that he decamped from the White Plains, and waited a mean opportunity to ravage the defenceless Jerseys; but it is great credit to us, that, with a handful of men, we sustained an orderly retreat for near an hundred miles, brought off our ammunition, all our field pieces, the greatest part of our stores, and had four rivers to pass. None can say that our retreat was precipitate, for we were near three weeks in performing it, that the country might have time to come in. Twice we marched back to meet the enemy, and remained out till dark. The sign of fear was not seen in our camp, and had

A militia infantryman in the Continental Army.

not some of the cowardly and disaffected inhabitants spread false alarms through the country, the Jerseys had never been ravaged. Once more we are again collected and collecting; our new army at both ends of the continent is recruiting fast, and we shall be able to open the next campaign with sixty thousand men, well armed and clothed. This is our situation, and who will may know it. By perseverance and fortitude we have the prospect of a glorious issue; by cowardice and submission, the sad choice of a variety of evils—a ravaged country—a depopulated city—habitations without safety, and slavery without hope—our homes turned into barracks and bawdy-houses for Hessians, and a future race to provide for, whose fathers we shall doubt of. Look on this picture and weep over it! and if there yet remains one thoughtless wretch who believes it not, let him suffer it unlamented.

* The present winter is worth an age, if rightly employed; but, if lost or neglected, the whole continent will partake of the evil; and there is no punishment that man does not deserve, be he who, or what, or where he will, that may be the means of sacrificing a season so precious and useful.

Yankee Doodle was first sung in the Colonies by British soldiers as a taunt to the Continentals—"doodle" was a term for a country bumpkin.

> Yankee Doodle came to town,
> For to buy a firelock;
> We will tar and feather him
> And so we will John Hancock.

However, the American militia latched onto the tune. By 1775, they sang it to the redcoats while forcing them back to Boston after Lexington and Concord. Following General Burgoyne's surrender on October 17, 1777, British officer Thomas Aubrey wrote: ". . . The (British) soldiers at Boston used it as a term of reproach, but after the affair at Bunker's Hill, the Americans gloried in it. Yankee Doodle is now their paean, a favourite of favourites, played in their army, esteemed as warlike as the Grenadier's March—it is the lover's spell, the nurse's lullaby . . . it was not a little mortifying to hear them play this tune, when their army marched down to our surrender."

Three boys circa 1965, reenacting the fife and drum corps of the Revolutionary War in celebration of American Independence.

Yankee Doodle

American

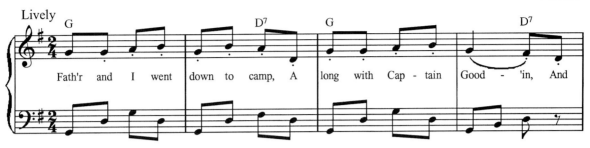

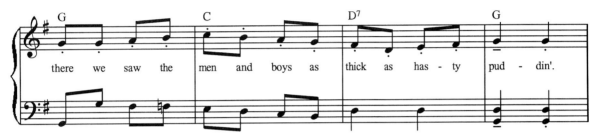

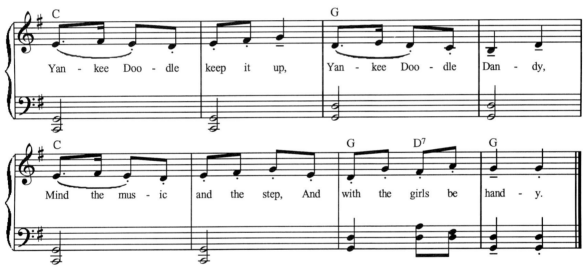

Yankee Doodle went to town,
A-riding on a pony;
Stuck a feather in his hat
and called it macaroni.
(CHORUS)
There was Captain Washington
Upon a slapping stallion,
A-giving orders to his men,
I guess there was a million.

(CHORUS)
We saw a little barrel, too,
The heads were made of leather;
They knocked upon it with little
 clubs,
And called the folks together.
(CHORUS)
And there they'd fife away like fun,
And play on cornstalk fiddles,
And some had ribbons red as blood,
All bound around their middles.

(CHORUS)
And then we saw a swamping gun,
Large as a log of maple;
Upon a deuced little cart,
A load for father's cattle.
(CHORUS)
And every time they shoot it off,
It takes a horn of powder;
It makes a noise like father's gun,
Only a nation louder.

PART II

DEFINING FREEDOM

THE ARTICLES OF CONFEDERATION

1777

To all to whom these Presents shall come, we the undersigned Delegates of the States affixed to our Names send greeting.

Articles of Confederation and perpetual Union between the states of New Hampshire, Massachusetts-bay, Rhode Island and Providence Plantations, Connecticut, New York, New Jersey, Pennsylvania, Delaware, Maryland, Virginia, North Carolina, South Carolina and Georgia.

I The Stile of this Confederacy shall be "The United States of America".

II Each state retains its sovereignty, freedom, and independence, and every power, jurisdiction, and right, which is not by this Confederation expressly delegated to the United States, in Congress assembled.

III The said States hereby severally enter into a firm league of friendship with each other, for their common defense, the security of their liberties, and their mutual and general welfare, binding themselves to assist each other, against all force offered to, or attacks made upon them, or any of them, on account of religion, sovereignty, trade, or any other pretense whatever.

IV The better to secure and perpetuate mutual friendship and intercourse among the people of the different States in this Union, the free inhabitants of each of these States, paupers, vagabonds, and fugitives from justice excepted, shall be entitled to all privileges and immunities of free citizens in the several States; and the people of each State shall free ingress and regress to and from any other State, and shall enjoy therein all the privileges of trade and commerce, subject to the same duties, impositions, and restrictions as the inhabitants thereof respectively, provided that such restrictions shall not extend so far as to prevent the removal of property imported into any State, to any other State, of which the owner is an inhabitant; provided also that no imposition, duties or restriction shall be laid by any State, on the property of the United States, or either of them.

If any person guilty of, or charged with, treason, felony, or other high misdemeanor in any State, shall flee from justice, and be found in any of the United States, he shall, upon demand of the Governor or executive power of the State from which he fled, be delivered up and removed to the State having jurisdiction of his offense. Full faith and credit shall be given in each of these States to the records, acts, and judicial proceedings of the courts and magistrates of every other State.

INDEPENDENCE HALL.
PHILADELPHIA 1876.

*An 1876 rendering of Independence Hall in Philadelphia, Pennsylvania, where the United States
Constitution was written, the Declaration of Independence was first read, and the Liberty Bell
was rung to acclaim its adoption. To the left is the Old City Hall where the Supreme Court
sat from 1790 until 1800 and to its right is Congress Hall where Congress sat from
1790 until 1800, while the city was the capital of the United States.*

V For the most convenient management of the general interests of the United States, delegates
shall be annually appointed in such manner as the legislatures of each State shall direct, to
meet in Congress on the first Monday in November, in every year, with a power reserved to
each State to recall its delegates, or any of them, at any time within the year, and to send others in their stead for the remainder of the year.

No State shall be represented in Congress by less than two, nor more than seven members; and
no person shall be capable of being a delegate for more than three years in any term of six years;

nor shall any person, being a delegate, be capable of holding any office under the United States, for which he, or another for his benefit, receives any salary, fees or emolument of any kind.

Each State shall maintain its own delegates in a meeting of the States, and while they act as members of the committee of the States.

In determining questions in the United States in Congress assembled, each State shall have one vote.

Freedom of speech and debate in Congress shall not be impeached or questioned in any court or place out of Congress, and the members of Congress shall be protected in their persons from arrests or imprisonments, during the time of their going to and from, and attendance on Congress, except for treason, felony, or breach of the peace.

VI No State, without the consent of the United States in Congress assembled, shall send any embassy to, or receive any embassy from, or enter into any conference, agreement, alliance or treaty with any King, Prince or State; nor shall any person holding any office of profit or trust under the United States, or any of them, accept any present, emolument, office or title of any kind whatever from any King, Prince or foreign State; nor shall the United States in Congress assembled, or any of them, grant any title of nobility.

No two or more States shall enter into any treaty, confederation or alliance whatever between them, without the consent of the United States in Congress assembled, specifying accurately the purposes for which the same is to be entered into, and how long it shall continue.

No State shall lay any imposts or duties, which may interfere with any stipulations in treaties, entered into by the United States in Congress assembled, with any King, Prince or State, in pursuance of any treaties already proposed by Congress, to the courts of France and Spain.

No vessel of war shall be kept up in time of peace by any State, except such number only, as shall be deemed necessary by the United States in Congress assembled, for the defense of such State, or its trade; nor shall any body of forces be kept up by any State in time of peace, except such number only, as in the judgement of the United States in Congress assembled, shall be deemed requisite to garrison the forts necessary for the defense of such State; but every State shall always keep up a well-regulated and disciplined militia, sufficiently armed and accoutered, and shall provide and constantly have ready for use, in public stores, a due number of filed pieces and tents, and a proper quantity of arms, ammunition and camp equipage.

No State shall engage in any war without the consent of the United States in Congress assembled, unless such State be actually invaded by enemies, or shall have received certain advice of a resolution being formed by some nation of Indians to invade such State, and the danger is so imminent as not to admit of a delay till the United States in Congress assembled can be consulted; nor shall any State grant commissions to any ships or vessels of war, nor letters of marque or reprisal, except it be after a declaration of war by the United States in Congress assembled, and then only against the Kingdom or State and the subjects thereof, against which war has been so declared, and under such regulations as shall be established by the United States in Congress assembled, unless such State be infested by pirates, in which case vessels of war may be fitted out for that occasion, and kept so long as the danger shall continue, or until the United States in Congress assembled shall determine otherwise.

VII When land forces are raised by any State for the common defense, all officers of or under the rank of colonel, shall be appointed by the legislature of each State respectively, by whom such forces shall be raised, or in such manner as such State shall direct, and all vacancies shall be filled up by the State which first made the appointment.

VIII All charges of war, and all other expenses that shall be incurred for the common defense or general welfare, and allowed by the United States in Congress assembled, shall be defrayed out of a common treasury, which shall be supplied by the several States in proportion to the value of all land within each State, granted or surveyed for any person, as such land and the buildings and improvements thereon shall be estimated according to such mode as the United States in Congress assembled, shall from time to time direct and appoint. The taxes for paying that proportion shall be laid and levied by the authority and direction of the legislatures of the several States within the time agreed upon by the United States in Congress assembled.

IX The United States in Congress assembled, shall have the sole and exclusive right and power of determining on peace and war, except in the cases mentioned in the sixth article — of sending and receiving ambassadors — entering into treaties and alliances, provided that no treaty of commerce shall be made whereby the legislative power of the respective States shall be restrained from imposing such imposts and duties on foreigners, as their own people are subjected to, or from prohibiting the exportation or importation of any species of goods or commodities whatsoever — of establishing rules for deciding in all cases, what captures on land or water shall be legal, and in what manner prizes taken by land or naval forces in the service of the United States shall be divided or appropriated — of granting letters of marque and reprisal in times of peace — appointing courts for the trial of piracies and felonies commited on the high seas and establishing courts for receiving and determining finally appeals in all cases of captures, provided that no member of Congress shall be appointed a judge of any of the said courts.

The United States in Congress assembled shall also be the last resort on appeal in all disputes and differences now subsisting or that hereafter may arise between two or more States concerning boundary, jurisdiction or any other causes whatever; which authority shall always be exercised in the manner following. Whenever the legislative or executive authority or lawful agent of any State in controversy with another shall present a petition to Congress stating the matter in question and praying for a hearing, notice thereof shall be given by order of Congress to the legislative or executive authority of the other State in controversy, and a day assigned for the appearance of the parties by their lawful agents, who shall then be directed to appoint by joint consent, commissioners or judges to constitute a court for hearing and determining the matter in question: but if they cannot agree, Congress shall name three persons out of each of the United States, and from the list of such persons each party shall alternately strike out one, the petitioners beginning, until the number shall be reduced to thirteen; and from that number not less than seven, nor more than nine names as Congress shall direct, shall in the presence

*A map of the United States of America after the Treaty of 1783, marking the
claims of the older States to the Western Lands.*

of Congress be drawn out by lot, and the persons whose names shall be so drawn or any five of them, shall be commissioners or judges, to hear and finally determine the controversy, so always as a major part of the judges who shall hear the cause shall agree in the determination: and if either party shall neglect to attend at the day appointed, without showing reasons, which Congress shall judge sufficient, or being present shall refuse to strike, the Congress shall proceed to nominate three persons out of each State, and the secretary of Congress shall strike in behalf of such party absent or refusing; and the judgement and sentence of the court to be appointed, in the manner before prescribed, shall be final and conclusive; and if any of the parties shall refuse to submit to the authority of such court, or to appear or defend their claim or cause, the court shall nevertheless proceed to pronounce sentence, or judgement, which shall in like manner be final and decisive, the judgement or sentence and other proceedings being in either case transmitted to Congress, and lodged among the acts of Congress for the security of the parties concerned: provided that every commissioner, before he sits in judgement, shall take an oath to be administered by one of the judges of the supreme or superior court of the State, where the cause shall be tried, 'well and truly to hear and determine the matter in question, according to the best of his judgement, without favor, affection or hope of reward': provided also, that no State shall be deprived of territory for the benefit of the United States.

All controversies concerning the private right of soil claimed under different grants of two or more States, whose jurisdictions as they may respect such lands, and the States which passed such grants are adjusted, the said grants or either of them being at the same time claimed to have originated antecedent to such settlement of jurisdiction, shall on the petition of either party to the Congress of the United States, be finally determined as near as may be in the same manner as is before prescribed for deciding disputes respecting territorial jurisdiction between different States.

The United States in Congress assembled shall also have the sole and exclusive right and power of regulating the alloy and value of coin struck by their own authority, or by that of the respective States — fixing the standards of weights and measures throughout the United States — regulating the trade and managing all affairs with the Indians, not members of any of the States, provided that the legislative right of any State within its own limits be not infringed or violated — establishing or regulating post offices from one State to another, throughout all the United States, and exacting such postage on the papers passing through the same as may be requisite to defray the expenses of the said office — appointing all officers of the land forces, in the service of the United States, excepting regimental officers — appointing all the officers of the naval forces, and commissioning all officers whatever in the service of the United States — making rules for the government and regulation of the said land and naval forces, and directing their operations. The United States in Congress assembled shall have authority to appoint a committee, to sit in the recess of Congress, to be denominated 'A Committee of the States', and to consist of one delegate from each State; and to appoint such other committees and civil officers as may be necessary for managing the general affairs of the United States under their direction — to appoint one of their members to preside, provided that no person be allowed to serve in the office of president more than one year in any term of three years; to ascertain the necessary sums of money to be raised for the service of the United States, and to appropriate and apply the same for defraying the public expenses — to borrow money, or emit bills on the credit of the United States, transmitting every half-year to the respective States an account of the sums of money so borrowed or emitted — to build and equip a navy — to agree upon the number of land forces, and to make requisitions from each State for its quota, in proportion to the number of white inhabitants in such State; which requisition shall be binding, and thereupon the legislature of each State shall appoint the regimental officers, raise the men and cloath, arm and equip them in a solid-like manner, at the expense of the United States; and the officers and men so cloathed, armed and equipped shall march to the place appointed, and within the time agreed on by the United States in Congress assembled. But if the United States in Congress assembled shall, on consideration of circumstances judge proper that any State should not raise men, or should raise a smaller number of men than the quota thereof, such extra number shall be raised, officered, cloathed, armed and equipped in the same manner as the quota of each State, unless the legislature of such State shall judge that such extra number cannot be safely spread out in the same, in which case they shall raise, officer, cloath, arm and equip as many of such extra number as they judge can be safely spared. And the officers and men so cloathed, armed, and equipped, shall march to the place appointed, and within the time agreed on by the United States in Congress assembled.

The United States in Congress assembled shall never engage in a war, nor grant letters of marque or reprisal in time of peace, nor enter into any treaties or alliances, nor coin money, nor regulate the value thereof, nor ascertain the sums and expenses necessary for the defense and welfare of the United States, or any of them, nor emit bills, nor borrow money on the credit of the United States, nor appropriate money, nor agree upon the number of vessels of war, to be built or purchased, or the number of land or sea forces to be raised, nor appoint a commander in chief of the army or navy, unless nine States assent to the same: nor shall a question on any other point, except for adjourning from day to day be determined, unless by the votes of the majority of the United States in Congress assembled. The Congress of the United States shall have power to adjourn to any time within the year, and to any place within the United States, so that no period of adjournment be for a longer duration than the space of six months, and shall publish the journal of their proceedings monthly, except such parts thereof relating to treaties, alliances or military operations, as in their judgement require secrecy; and the yeas and nays of the delegates of each State on any question shall be entered on the journal, when it is desired by any delegates of a State, or any of them, at his or their request shall be furnished with a transcript of the said journal, except such parts as are above excepted, to lay before the legislatures of the several States.

X The Committee of the States, or any nine of them, shall be authorized to execute, in the recess of Congress, such of the powers of Congress as the United States in Congress assembled, by the consent of the nine States, shall from time to time think expedient to vest them with; provided that no power be delegated to the said Committee, for the exercise of which, by the Articles of Confederation, the voice of nine States in the Congress of the United States assembled be requisite.

XI Canada acceding to this confederation, and adjoining in the measures of the United States, shall be admitted into, and entitled to all the advantages of this Union; but no other colony shall be admitted into the same, unless such admission be agreed to by nine States.

XII All bills of credit emitted, monies borrowed, and debts contracted by, or under the authority of Congress, before the assembling of the United States, in pursuance of the present confederation, shall be deemed and considered as a charge against the United States, for payment and satisfaction whereof the said United States, and the public faith are hereby solemnly pleged.

XIII Every State shall abide by the determination of the United States in Congress assembled, on all questions which by this confederation are submitted to them. And the Articles of this Confederation shall be inviolably observed by every State, and the Union shall be perpetual; nor shall any alteration at any time hereafter be made in any of them; unless such alteration be agreed to in a Congress of the United States, and be afterwards confirmed by the legislatures of every State.

Three Great Men, 1790, a painting by Constantino Brumidi. President George Washington in consultation with his Secretary of State Thomas Jefferson and Secretary of the Treasury Alexander Hamilton.

And Whereas it hath pleased the Great Governor of the World to incline the hearts of the legislatures we respectively represent in Congress, to approve of, and to authorize us to ratify the said Articles of Confederation and perpetual Union. Know Ye that we the undersigned delegates, by virtue of the power and authority to us given for that purpose, do by these presents, in the name and in behalf of our respective constituents, fully and entirely ratify and confirm each and every of the said Articles of Confederation and perpetual Union, and all and singular the matters and things therein contained: And we do further solemnly plight and engage the faith of our respective constituents, that they shall abide by the determinations of the United States in Congress assembled, on all questions, which by the said Confederation are submitted to them. And that the Articles thereof shall be inviolably observed by the States we respectively represent, and that the Union shall be perpetual.

In Witness whereof we have hereunto set our hands in Congress. Done at Philadelphia in the State of Pennsylvania the ninth day of July in the Year of our Lord One Thousand Seven Hundred and Seventy-Eight, and in the Third Year of the independence of America.

Agreed to by Congress 15 November 1777. In force after ratification by Maryland, 1 March 1781.

FEDERALIST No. 1

Alexander Hamilton, 1787

To the People of the State of New York: General Introduction for the Independent Journal.

After an unequivocal experience of the inefficiency of the subsisting federal government, you are called upon to deliberate on a new Constitution for the United States of America. The subject speaks its own importance; comprehending in its consequences nothing less than the existence of the UNION, the safety and welfare of the parts of which it is composed, the fate of an empire in many respects the most interesting in the world. It has been frequently remarked that it seems to have been reserved to the people of this country, by their conduct and example, to decide the important question, whether societies of men are really capable or not of establishing good government from reflection and choice, or whether they are forever destined to depend for their political constitutions on accident and force. If there be any truth in the remark, the crisis at which we are arrived may with propriety be regarded as the era in which that decision is to be made; and a wrong election of the part we shall act may, in this view, deserve to be considered as the general misfortune of mankind. This idea will add the inducements of philanthropy to those of patriotism, to heighten the solicitude which all considerate and good men must feel for the event. Happy will it be if our choice should be directed by a judicious estimate of our true interests, unperplexed and unbiased by considerations not connected with the public good. But this is a thing more ardently to be wished than seriously to be expected. The plan offered to our deliberations affects too many particular interests, innovates upon too many local institutions, not to involve in its discussion a variety of objects foreign to its merits, and of views, passions and prejudices little favorable to the discovery of truth. Among the most formidable of the obstacles which the new Constitution will have to encounter may readily be distinguished the obvious interest of a certain class of men in every State to resist all changes which may

American statesman Alexander Hamilton (1757–1804), the author of the majority of the Federalist Papers. He became President Washington's Secretary of the Treasury.

hazard a diminution of the power, emolument, and consequence of the offices they hold under the State establish-
ments; and the perverted ambition of another class of men,
who will either hope to aggrandize themselves by the confu-
sions of their country, or will flatter themselves with fairer
prospects of elevation from the subdivision of the empire
into several partial confederacies than from its union under
one government. It is not, however, my design to dwell upon
observations of this nature. I am well aware that it would be
disingenuous to resolve indiscriminately the opposition of
any set of men (merely because their situations might subject them to suspicion) into interested or ambitious views.
Candor will oblige us to admit that even such men may be
actuated by upright intentions; and it cannot be doubted
that much of the opposition which has made its appearance,
or may hereafter make its appearance, will spring from
sources, blameless at least, if not respectable—the honest
errors of minds led astray by preconceived jealousies and
fears. So numerous indeed and so powerful are the causes
which serve to give a false bias to the judgment, that we,
upon many occasions, see wise and good men on the wrong
as well as on the right side of questions of the first magnitude to society. This circumstance, if duly attended to, would
furnish a lesson of moderation to those who are ever so
much persuaded of their being in the right in any controversy. And a further reason for caution, in this respect, might be
drawn from the reflection that we are not always sure that
those who advocate the truth are influenced by purer principles than their antagonists. Ambition, avarice, personal ani-
mosity, party opposition, and many other motives not more
laudable than these, are apt to operate as well upon those
who support as those who oppose the right side of a question. Were there not even these inducements to moderation,
nothing could be more ill-judged than that intolerant spirit
which has, at all times, characterized political parties. For in
politics, as in religion, it is equally absurd to aim at making
proselytes by fire and sword. Heresies in either can rarely be
cured by persecution.

On September 16, 1787, the delegates who signed the draft of the Constitution in Philadelphia stipulated that it would take effect only after being ratified at conventions in nine of the thirteen states. Because of their size and power, either of two key states, New York or Virginia, could destroy the whole enter-prise with a negative vote. Both states' delegates were sharply divided in their opinions of the Constitution, and New York's governor had made it clear that he was against it.

Alexander Hamilton of New York, one of Washington's aides during the Revolution, asked James Madison of Virginia to join him in a crucial project. The purpose: to persuade the New York convention to ratify the Constitution. The method: writing a series of letters to New York newspapers, in which they would explain and defend the Constitution under a shared pseudonym, "Publius." Hamilton outlined the sequence of topics and vigorously addressed most of them in 51 of the let-ters—sometimes writing four essays in a single week. Madison's 29 letters were memorable in their combination of frankness, balance, and reasoning power. John Jay, an older scholar from New York, later named as first Chief Justice of the Supreme Court, assisted by writ-ing five.

It is not certain that *The Federalist Papers*, written between October 1787 and May 1788, made the final difference in New York's grudging ratification of the Constitution. But there is no doubt that it remains a most authoritative work of political philosophy and pragmatic gov-ernment. Thomas Jefferson called *The Federalist Papers*, " . . . the best com-mentary on the principles of government . . . ever written," and it has been com-pared to Plato's *Republic*, Aristotle's *Politics*, and Hobbes' *Leviathan*.

And yet, however just these sentiments will be allowed to be, we have already sufficient indications that it will happen in this as in all former cases of great national discussion. A torrent of angry and malignant passions will be let loose. To judge from the conduct of the opposite parties, we shall be led to conclude that they will mutually hope to evince the justness of their opinions, and to increase the number of their converts by the loudness of their declamations and the bitterness of their invectives. An enlightened zeal for the energy and efficiency of government will be stigmatized as the offspring of a temper fond of despotic power and hostile to the principles of liberty. An over-scrupulous jealousy of danger to the rights of the people, which is more commonly the fault of the head than of the heart, will be represented as mere pretense and artifice, the stale bait for popularity at the expense of the public good. It will be forgotten, on the one hand, that jealousy is the usual concomitant of love, and that the noble enthusiasm of liberty is apt to be infected with a spirit of narrow and illiberal distrust. On the other hand, it will be equally forgotten that the vigor of government is essential to the security of liberty; that, in the contemplation of a sound and well-informed judgment, their interest can never be separated; and that a dangerous ambition more often lurks behind the specious mask of zeal for the rights of the people than under the forbidden appearance of zeal for the firmness and efficiency of government. History will teach us that the former has been found a much more certain road to the introduction of despotism than the latter, and that of those men who have overturned the liberties of republics, the greatest number have begun their career by paying an obsequious court to the people; commencing demagogues, and ending tyrants.

In the course of the preceding observations, I have had an eye, my fellow-citizens, to putting you upon your guard against all attempts, from whatever quarter, to influence your decision in a matter of the utmost moment to your welfare, by any impressions other than those which may result from the evidence of truth. You will, no doubt, at the same time, have collected from the general scope of them, that they proceed from a source not unfriendly to the new Constitution. Yes, my countrymen, I own to you that, after having given it an attentive consideration, I am clearly of opinion it is your interest to adopt it. I am convinced that this is the safest course for your liberty, your dignity, and your happiness. I affect not reserves which I do not feel. I will not amuse you with an appearance of deliberation when I have decided. I frankly acknowledge to you my convictions, and I will freely lay before you the reasons on which they are founded. The consciousness of good intentions disdains ambiguity. I shall not, however, multiply professions on this head. My motives must remain in the depository of my own breast. My arguments will be open to all, and may be judged of by all. They shall at least be offered in a spirit which will not disgrace the cause of truth.

OLD GLORY ALOFT

By Frank Lebby Stanton

She's up there, — Old Glory, — where lightnings are sped;

She dazzles the nations with ripples of red;

And she'll wave for us living, or droop o'er us dead, —

The flag of our country forever!

She's up there, — Old Glory, — how bright the stars stream!

And the stripes like red signals of light are agleam!

And we dare for her, living, or dream the last dream,

'Neath the flag of our country forever!

She's up there, — Old Glory, — no tyrant-dealt scars,

No blur on her brightness, no stain on her stars!

The brave blood of heroes hath crimsoned her bars.

She's the flag of our country forever!

CONSTITUTION OF THE
UNITED STATES OF AMERICA

1787

Preamble

We the People of the United States, in Order to form a more perfect Union, establish Justice, insure domestic Tranquility, provide for the common defence, promote the general Welfare, and secure the Blessings of Liberty to ourselves and our Posterity, do ordain and establish this Constitution for the United States of America.

Article I

Section 1.
All legislative Powers herein granted shall be vested in a Congress of the United States, which shall consist of a Senate and House of Representatives.

Section 2.
The House of Representatives shall be composed of Members chosen every second Year by the People of the several States, and the Electors in each State shall have the Qualifications requisite for Electors of the most numerous Branch of the State Legislature.

No Person shall be a Representative who shall not have attained to the Age of twenty five Years, and been seven Years a Citizen of the United States, and who shall not, when elected, be an Inhabitant of that State in which he shall be chosen.

Representatives and direct Taxes shall be apportioned among the several States which may be included within this Union, according to their respective Numbers, which shall be determined by adding to the whole Number of free Persons, including those bound to Service for a Term of Years, and excluding Indians not taxed, three fifths of all other Persons. The actual Enumeration shall be made within three Years after the first Meeting of the Congress of the United States, and within every subsequent Term of ten Years, in such Manner as they shall by Law direct. The Number of Representatives shall not exceed one for every thirty Thousand, but each State shall have at Least one Representative; and until such enumeration shall be made, the State of New Hampshire shall be entitled to chuse three, Massachusetts eight, Rhode-Island and Providence Plantations one, Connecticut five, New-York six, New Jersey four, Pennsylvania eight, Delaware one, Maryland six, Virginia ten, North Carolina five, South Carolina five, and Georgia three.

When vacancies happen in the Representation from any State, the Executive Authority thereof shall issue Writs of Election to fill such Vacancies.

*A painting of the Constitution Assembly that was called to decide the final
form of the American Constitution.*

The House of Representatives shall chuse their Speaker and other Officers; and shall have the sole Power of Impeachment.

Section 3.
The Senate of the United States shall be composed of two Senators from each State, chosen by the Legislature thereof, for six Years; and each Senator shall have one Vote.

Immediately after they shall be assembled in Consequence of the first Election, they shall be divided as equally as may be into three Classes. The Seats of the Senators of the first Class shall be vacated at the Expiration of the second Year, of the second Class at the Expiration of the fourth Year, and of the third Class at the Expiration of the sixth Year, so that one third may be chosen every second Year; and if Vacancies happen by Resignation, or otherwise, during the Recess of the Legislature of any State, the Executive thereof may make temporary Appointments until the next Meeting of the Legislature, which shall then fill such Vacancies.

No Person shall be a Senator who shall not have attained to the Age of thirty Years, and been nine Years a Citizen of the United States, and who shall not, when elected, be an Inhabitant of that State for which he shall be chosen.

The Vice President of the United States shall be President of the Senate, but shall have no Vote, unless they be equally divided.

The Senate shall chuse their other Officers, and also a President pro tempore, in the Absence of the Vice President, or when he shall exercise the Office of President of the United States.

The Senate shall have the sole Power to try all Impeachments. When sitting for that Purpose, they shall be on Oath or Affirmation. When the President of the United States is tried the Chief Justice shall preside: And no Person shall be convicted without the Concurrence of two thirds of the Members present.

Judgment in Cases of Impeachment shall not extend further than to removal from Office, and disqualification to hold and enjoy any Office of honor, Trust or Profit under the United States: but the Party convicted shall nevertheless be liable and subject to Indictment, Trial, Judgment and Punishment, according to Law.

A scene of New Hampshire.

Section 4.
The Times, Places and Manner of holding Elections for Senators and Representatives, shall be prescribed in each State by the Legislature thereof; but the Congress may at any time by Law make or alter such Regulations, except as to the Places of chusing Senators.

The Congress shall assemble at least once in every Year, and such Meeting shall be on the first Monday in December, unless they shall by Law appoint a different Day.

Section 5.
Each House shall be the Judge of the Elections, Returns and Qualifications of its own Members, and a Majority of each shall constitute a Quorum to do Business; but a smaller Number may adjourn from day to day, and may be authorized to compel the Attendance of absent Members, in such Manner, and under such Penalties as each House may provide.

Each House may determine the Rules of its Proceedings, punish its Members for disorderly Behaviour, and, with the Concurrence of two thirds, expel a Member.

Each House shall keep a Journal of its Proceedings, and from time to time publish the same, excepting such Parts as may in their Judgment require Secrecy; and the Yeas and Nays of the Members of either House on any question shall, at the Desire of one fifth of those Present, be entered on the Journal.

Neither House, during the Session of Congress, shall, without the Consent of the other, adjourn for more than three days, nor to any other Place than that in which the two Houses shall be sitting.

Section 6.
The Senators and Representatives shall receive a Compensation for their Services, to be ascertained by Law, and paid out of the Treasury of the United States. They shall in all Cases, except Treason, Felony and Breach of the Peace, be privileged from Arrest during their

Attendance at the Session of their respective Houses, and in going to and returning from the same; and for any Speech or Debate in either House, they shall not be questioned in any other Place.

No Senator or Representative shall, during the Time for which he was elected, be appointed to any civil Office under the Authority of the United States, which shall have been created, or the Emoluments whereof shall have been encreased during such time; and no Person holding any Office under the United States, shall be a Member of either House during his Continuance in Office.

Section 7.

All Bills for raising Revenue shall originate in the House of Representatives; but the Senate may propose or concur with Amendments as on other Bills.

Every Bill which shall have passed the House of Representatives and the Senate, shall, before it become a Law, be presented to the President of the United States; If he approve he shall sign it, but if not he shall return it, with his Objections to that House in which it shall have originated, who shall enter the Objections at large on their Journal, and proceed to reconsider it. If after such Reconsideration two thirds of that House shall agree to pass the Bill, it shall be sent, together with the Objections, to the other House, by which it shall likewise be reconsidered, and if approved by two thirds of that House, it shall become a Law. But in all such Cases the Votes of both Houses shall be determined by yeas and Nays, and the Names of the Persons voting for and against the Bill shall be entered on the Journal of each House respectively. If any Bill shall not be returned by the President within ten Days (Sundays excepted) after it shall have been presented to him, the Same shall be a Law, in like Manner as if he had signed it, unless the Congress by their Adjournment prevent its Return, in which Case it shall not be a Law.

Every Order, Resolution, or Vote to which the Concurrence of the Senate and House of Representatives may be necessary (except on a question of Adjournment) shall be presented to the President of the United States; and before the Same shall take Effect, shall be approved by him, or being disapproved by him, shall be repassed by two thirds of the Senate and House of Representatives, according to the Rules and Limitations prescribed in the Case of a Bill.

Section 8.

The Congress shall have Power To lay and collect Taxes, Duties, Imposts and Excises, to pay the Debts and provide for the common Defence and general Welfare of the United States; but all Duties, Imposts and Excises shall be uniform throughout the United States;

Cape Ann, Massachusetts.

Mystic, Connecticut.

To borrow Money on the credit of the United States;

To regulate Commerce with foreign Nations, and among the several States, and with the Indian Tribes;

To establish an uniform Rule of Naturalization, and uniform Laws on the subject of Bankruptcies throughout the United States;

To coin Money, regulate the Value thereof, and of foreign Coin, and fix the Standard of Weights and Measures;

To provide for the Punishment of counterfeiting the Securities and current Coin of the United States;

To establish Post Offices and Post Roads;

To promote the Progress of Science and useful Arts, by securing for limited Times to Authors and Inventors the exclusive Right to their respective Writings and Discoveries;

To constitute Tribunals inferior to the supreme Court;

To define and punish Piracies and Felonies committed on the high Seas, and Offences against the Law of Nations;

To declare War, grant Letters of Marque and Reprisal, and make Rules concerning Captures on Land and Water;

To raise and support Armies, but no Appropriation of Money to that Use shall be for a longer Term than two Years;

To provide and maintain a Navy;

To make Rules for the Government and Regulation of the land and naval Forces;

To provide for calling forth the Militia to execute the Laws of the Union, suppress Insurrections and repel Invasions;

To provide for organizing, arming, and disciplining, the Militia, and for governing such Part of them as may be employed in the Service of the United States, reserving to the States respectively, the Appointment of the Officers, and the Authority of training the Militia according to the discipline prescribed by Congress;

To exercise exclusive Legislation in all Cases whatsoever, over such District (not exceeding ten Miles square) as may, by Cession of particular States, and the Acceptance of Congress, become the Seat of the Government of the United States, and to exercise like Authority over all Places purchased by the Consent of the Legislature of the State in which the Same shall be, for the Erection of Forts, Magazines, Arsenals, dock-Yards, and other needful Buildings;—And

To make all Laws which shall be necessary and proper for carrying into Execution the foregoing Powers, and all other Powers vested by this Constitution in the Government of the United States, or in any Department or Officer thereof.

Section. 9.

The Migration or Importation of such Persons as any of the States now existing shall think proper to admit, shall not be prohibited by the Congress prior to the Year one thousand eight hundred and eight, but a Tax or duty may be imposed on such Importation, not exceeding ten dollars for each Person.

The Privilege of the Writ of Habeas Corpus shall not be suspended, unless when in Cases of Rebellion or Invasion the public Safety may require it.

No Bill of Attainder or ex post facto Law shall be passed.

No Capitation, or other direct, Tax shall be laid, unless in Proportion to the Census or Enumeration herein before directed to be taken.

No Tax or Duty shall be laid on Articles exported from any State.

No Preference shall be given by any Regulation of Commerce or Revenue to the Ports of one State over those of another: nor shall Vessels bound to, or from, one State, be obliged to enter, clear, or pay Duties in another.

Niagara Falls, New York.

No Money shall be drawn from the Treasury, but in Consequence of Appropriations made by Law; and a regular Statement and Account of the Receipts and Expenditures of all public Money shall be published from time to time.

No Title of Nobility shall be granted by the United States: And no Person holding any Office of Profit or Trust under them, shall, without the Consent of the Congress, accept of any present, Emolument, Office, or Title, of any kind whatever, from any King, Prince, or foreign State.

Section 10.

No State shall enter into any Treaty, Alliance, or Confederation; grant Letters of Marque and Reprisal; coin Money; emit Bills of Credit; make any Thing but gold and silver Coin a Tender in Payment of Debts; pass any Bill of Attainder, ex post facto Law, or Law impairing the Obligation of Contracts, or grant any Title of Nobility.

No State shall, without the Consent of the Congress, lay any Imposts or Duties on Imports or Exports, except what may be absolutely necessary for executing its inspection Laws: and the net Produce of all Duties and Imposts, laid by any State on Imports or Exports, shall be for the

Use of the Treasury of the United States; and all such Laws shall be subject to the Revision and Controul of the Congress.

No State shall, without the Consent of Congress, lay any Duty of Tonnage, keep Troops, or Ships of War in time of Peace, enter into any Agreement or Compact with another State, or with a foreign Power, or engage in War, unless actually invaded, or in such imminent Danger as will not admit of delay.

Article II

Section 1.

The executive Power shall be vested in a President of the United States of America. He shall hold his Office during the Term of four Years, and, together with the Vice President, chosen for the same Term, be elected, as follows:

Each State shall appoint, in such Manner as the Legislature thereof may direct, a Number of Electors, equal to the whole Number of Senators and Representatives to which the State may be entitled in the Congress: but no Senator or Representative, or Person holding an Office of Trust or Profit under the United States, shall be appointed an Elector.

The Electors shall meet in their respective States, and vote by Ballot for two Persons, of whom one at least shall not be an Inhabitant of the same State with themselves. And they shall make a List of all the Persons voted for, and of the Number of Votes for each; which List they shall sign and certify, and transmit sealed to the Seat of Government of the United States, directed to the President of the Senate. The President of the Senate shall, in the Presence of the Senate and House of Representatives, open all the Certificates, and the Votes shall then be counted. The Person having the greatest Number of Votes shall be the President, if such Number be a Majority of the whole Number of Electors appointed; and if there be more than one who have such Majority, and have an equal Number of Votes, then the House of Representatives shall immediately chuse by Ballot one of them for President; and if no Person have a Majority, then from the five highest on the List the said House shall in like Manner chuse the President. But in chusing the President, the Votes shall be taken by States, the Representation from each State having one Vote; a quorum for this Purpose shall consist of a Member or Members from two thirds of the States, and a Majority of all the States shall be necessary to a Choice. In every Case, after the Choice of the President, the Person having the greatest Number of Votes of the Electors shall be the Vice President. But if there should remain two or more who have equal Votes, the

Philadelphia, Pennsylvania skyline.

Senate shall chuse from them by Ballot the Vice President.

The Congress may determine the Time of chusing the Electors, and the Day on which they shall give their Votes; which Day shall be the same throughout the United States.

No Person except a natural born Citizen, or a Citizen of the United States, at the time of the Adoption of this Constitution, shall be eligible to the Office of President; neither shall any Person be eligible to that Office who shall not have attained to the Age of thirty five Years, and been fourteen Years a Resident within the United States.

A harbor in Rhode Island.

In Case of the Removal of the President from Office, or of his Death, Resignation, or Inability to discharge the Powers and Duties of the said Office, the Same shall devolve on the Vice President, and the Congress may by Law provide for the Case of Removal, Death, Resignation or Inability, both of the President and Vice President declaring what Officer shall then act as President, and such Officer shall act accordingly, until the Disability be removed, or a President shall be elected.

The President shall, at stated Times, receive for his Services, a Compensation, which shall neither be encreased nor diminished during the Period for which he shall have been elected, and he shall not receive within that Period any other Emolument from the United States, or any of them.

Before he enter on the Execution of his Office, he shall take the following Oath or Affirmation:—"I do solemnly swear (or affirm) that I will faithfully execute the Office of President of the United States, and will to the best of my Ability, preserve, protect and defend the Constitution of the United States."

Section 2.
The President shall be Commander in Chief of the Army and Navy of the United States, and of the Militia of the several States, when called into the actual Service of the United States; he may require the Opinion, in writing, of the principal Officer in each of the executive Departments, upon any Subject relating to the Duties of their respective Offices, and he shall have Power to grant Reprieves and Pardons for Offences against the United States, except in Cases of Impeachment.

He shall have Power, by and with the Advice and Consent of the Senate, to make Treaties, provided two thirds of the Senators present concur; and he shall nominate, and by and with the Advice and Consent of the Senate, shall appoint Ambassadors, other public Ministers and Consuls, Judges of the supreme Court, and all other Officers of the United States, whose

Appointments are not herein otherwise provided for, and which shall be established by Law: but the Congress may by Law vest the Appointment of such inferior Officers, as they think proper, in the President alone, in the Courts of Law, or in the Heads of Departments.

The President shall have Power to fill up all Vacancies that may happen during the Recess of the Senate, by granting Commissions which shall expire at the End of their next Session.

Section 3.

He shall from time to time give to the Congress Information of the State of the Union, and recommend to their Consideration such Measures as he shall judge necessary and expedient; he may, on extraordinary Occasions, convene both Houses, or either of them, and in Case of Disagreement between them, with Respect to the Time of Adjournment, he may adjourn them to such Time as he shall think proper; he shall receive Ambassadors and other public Ministers; he shall take Care that the Laws be faithfully executed, and shall Commission all the Officers of the United States.

Blue Ridge Mountains, Virginia.

Section 4.

The President, Vice President and all civil Officers of the United States, shall be removed from Office on Impeachment for, and Conviction of, Treason, Bribery, or other high Crimes and Misdemeanors.

Article III

Section 1.

The judicial Power of the United States, shall be vested in one supreme Court, and in such inferior Courts as the Congress may from time to time ordain and establish. The Judges, both of the supreme and inferior Courts, shall hold their Offices during good Behaviour, and shall, at stated Times, receive for their Services, a Compensation which shall not be diminished during their Continuance in Office.

Section 2.

The judicial Power shall extend to all Cases, in Law and Equity, arising under this Constitution, the Laws of the United States, and Treaties made, or which shall be made, under their Authority;—to all Cases affecting Ambassadors, other public Ministers and Consuls;—to all Cases of admiralty and maritime Jurisdiction;—to Controversies to which the United States shall be a Party;—to Controversies between two or more States;—between a State and Citizens of another State;—between Citizens of different States,—between Citizens of the same State claiming Lands under Grants of different States, and between a State, or the Citizens thereof, and foreign States, Citizens or Subjects.

In all Cases affecting Ambassadors, other public Ministers and Consuls, and those in which a

State shall be Party, the supreme Court shall have original Jurisdiction. In all the other Cases before mentioned, the supreme Court shall have appellate Jurisdiction, both as to Law and Fact, with such Exceptions, and under such Regulations as the Congress shall make.

The Trial of all Crimes, except in Cases of Impeachment, shall be by Jury; and such Trial shall be held in the State where the said Crimes shall have been committed; but when not committed within any State, the Trial shall be at such Place or Places as the Congress may by Law have directed.

Section 3.

Treason against the United States, shall consist only in levying War against them, or in adhering to their Enemies, giving them Aid and Comfort. No Person shall be convicted of Treason unless on the Testimony of two Witnesses to the same overt Act, or on Confession in open Court.

The Congress shall have Power to declare the Punishment of Treason, but no Attainder of Treason shall work Corruption of Blood, or Forfeiture except during the Life of the Person attainted.

Article IV

Boone Hall Plantation, South Carolina.

Section 1.

Full Faith and Credit shall be given in each State to the public Acts, Records, and judicial Proceedings of every other State. And the Congress may by general Laws prescribe the Manner in which such Acts, Records and Proceedings shall be proved, and the Effect thereof.

Section 2.

The Citizens of each State shall be entitled to all Privileges and Immunities of Citizens in the several States.

A Person charged in any State with Treason, Felony, or other Crime, who shall flee from Justice, and be found in another State, shall on Demand of the executive Authority of the State from which he fled, be delivered up, to be removed to the State having Jurisdiction of the Crime.

No Person held to Service or Labour in one State, under the Laws thereof, escaping into another, shall, in Consequence of any Law or Regulation therein, be discharged from such Service or Labour, but shall be delivered up on Claim of the Party to whom such Service or Labour may be due.

Section 3.

New States may be admitted by the Congress into this Union; but no new State shall be formed or erected within the Jurisdiction of any other State; nor any State be formed by the Junction of two or more States, or Parts of States, without the Consent of the Legislatures of the States concerned as well as of the Congress.

The Congress shall have Power to dispose of and make all needful Rules and Regulations respecting the Territory or other Property belonging to the United States; and nothing in this Constitution shall be so construed as to Prejudice any Claims of the United States, or of any particular State.

Section 4.
The United States shall guarantee to every State in this Union a Republican Form of Government, and shall protect each of them against Invasion; and on Application of the Legislature, or of the Executive (when the Legislature cannot be convened) against domestic Violence.

Article V

The Congress, whenever two thirds of both Houses shall deem it necessary, shall propose Amendments to this Constitution, or, on the Application of the Legislatures of two thirds of the several States, shall call a Convention for proposing Amendments, which, in either Case, shall be valid to all Intents and Purposes, as Part of this Constitution, when ratified by the Legislatures of three fourths of the several States, or by Conventions in three fourths thereof, as the one or the other Mode of Ratification may be proposed by the Congress; Provided that no Amendment which may be made prior to the Year One thousand eight hundred and eight shall in any Manner affect the first and fourth Clauses in the Ninth Section of the first Article; and that no State, without its Consent, shall be deprived of its equal Suffrage in the Senate.

A harbor in Baltimore, Maryland.

Article VI

All Debts contracted and Engagements entered into, before the Adoption of this Constitution, shall be as valid against the United States under this Constitution, as under the Confederation.

This Constitution, and the Laws of the United States which shall be made in Pursuance thereof; and all Treaties made or which shall be made, under the Authority of the United States, shall be the supreme Law of the Land; and the Judges in every State shall be bound thereby, any Thing in the Constitution or Laws of any State to the Contrary notwithstanding.

The Senators and Representatives before mentioned, and the Members of the several State Legislatures, and all executive and judicial Officers, both of the United States and of the several States, shall be bound by Oath or Affirmation, to support this Constitution; but no religious Test shall ever be required as a Qualification to any Office or public Trust under the United States.

Article VII

The Ratification of the Conventions of nine States, shall be sufficient for the Establishment of this Constitution between the States so ratifying the Same.

Done in Convention by the Unanimous Consent of the States present the Seventeenth Day of September in the Year of our Lord one thousand seven hundred and Eighty seven and of the Independence of the United States of America the Twelfth. IN WITNESS whereof We have hereunto subscribed our Names,

Attest: William Jackson, Secretary

George Washington President and Deputy from Virginia

NEW HAMPSHIRE	John Langdon	DELAWARE	George Read
	Nicholas Gilman		Gunning Bedford, Jr.
MASSACHUSETTS	Nathaniel Gorham		John Dickinson
	Rufus King		Richard Bassett
CONNECTICUT	Wm. Samuel Johnson		Jacob Broom
	Roger Sherman	MARYLAND	James McHenry
NEW YORK	Alexander Hamilton		Dan of St. Thomas Jenifer
NEW JERSEY	William Livingston		Daniel Carroll
	David Brearley	VIRGINIA	John Blair
	William Paterson		James Madison, Jr.
	Jonathan Dayton	NORTH CAROLINA	William Blount
PENNSYLVANIA	Benjamin Franklin		Richard Dobbs Spaight
	Thomas Mifflin		Hugh Williamson
	Robert Morris	SOUTH CAROLINA	John Rutledge
	George Clymer		Charles Cotesworth Pinckney
	Thomas Fitzsimons		Charles Pinckney Pierce Butler
	Jared Ingersoll	GEORGIA	William Few
	James Wilson		Abraham Baldwin
	Gouverneur Morris		

Statue of Thomas Jefferson in the Jefferson Memorial. He was the primary author of the Bill of Rights.

THE BILL OF RIGHTS

AMENDMENTS TO THE U.S. CONSTITUTION, 1789

1. Congress shall make no law respecting an establishment of religion, or prohibiting the free exercise thereof; or abridging the freedom of speech, or of the press; or the right of the people peaceably to assemble, and to petition the government for a redress of grievances.

2. A well regulated Militia, being necessary to the security of a free State, the right of the people to keep and bear Arms, shall not be infringed.

3. No Soldier shall, in time of peace be quartered in any house, without the consent of the Owner, nor in time of war, but in a manner to be prescribed by law.

4. The right of the people to be secure in their persons, houses, papers, and effects, against unreasonable searches and seizures, shall not be violated, and no Warrants shall issue, but upon probable cause, supported by Oath or affirmation, and particularly describing the place to be searched, and the persons or things to be seized.

5. No person shall be held to answer for a capital, or otherwise infamous crime, unless on a presentment or indictment of a Grand Jury, except in cases arising in the land or naval forces, or in the Militia, when in actual service in time of War or public danger; nor shall any person be subject for the same offence to be twice put in jeopardy of life or limb; nor shall be compelled in any criminal case to be a witness against himself, nor be deprived of life, liberty, or property, without due process of law; nor shall private property be taken for public use, without just compensation.

6. In all criminal prosecutions, the accused shall enjoy the right to a speedy and public trial, by an impartial jury of the State and district wherein the crime shall have been committed, which district shall have been previously ascertained by law, and to be informed of the nature and cause of the accusation; to be confronted with the witnesses against him; to have compulsory process for obtaining witnesses in his favor, and to have the Assistance of Counsel for his defence.

7. In Suits at common law, where the value in controversy shall exceed twenty dollars, the right of trial by jury shall be preserved, and no fact tried by a jury, shall be otherwise re-examined in any Court of the United States, than according to the rules of the common law.

8. Excessive bail shall not be required, nor excessive fines imposed, nor cruel and unusual punishments inflicted.

9. The enumeration in the Constitution, of certain rights, shall not be construed to deny or disparage others retained by the people.

10. The powers not delegated to the United States by the Constitution, nor prohibited by it to the States, are reserved to the States respectively, or to the people.

The Ten Original Amendments: The Bill of Rights. Passed by Congress September 25, 1789. Ratified December 15, 1791.

Further amendments to the Constitution

11. The Judicial power of the United States shall not be construed to extend to any suit in law or equity, commenced or prosecuted against one of the United States by Citizens of another State, or by Citizens or Subjects of any Foreign State.
Passed by Congress March 4, 1794. Ratified February 7, 1795.

12. The Electors shall meet in their respective states, and vote by ballot for President and Vice-President, one of whom, at least, shall not be an inhabitant of the same state with themselves; they shall name in their ballots the person voted for as President, and in distinct ballots the person voted for as Vice-President, and they shall make distinct lists of all persons voted for as President, and of all persons voted for as Vice-President and of the number of votes for each, which lists they shall sign and certify, and transmit sealed to the seat of the government of the United States, directed to the President of the Senate;—The President of the Senate shall, in the presence of the Senate and House of Representatives, open all the certificates and the votes shall then be counted;—The person having the greatest number of votes for President, shall be the President, if such number be a majority of the whole number of Electors appointed; and if no person have such majority, then from the persons having the highest numbers not exceeding three on the list of those voted for as President, the House of Representatives shall choose immediately, by ballot, the President. But in choosing the President, the votes shall be taken by states, the representation from each state having one vote; a quorum for this purpose shall consist of a member or members from two-thirds of the states, and a majority of all the states shall be necessary to a choice. And if the House of Representatives shall not choose a President whenever the right of choice shall devolve upon them, before the fourth day of March next following, then the Vice-President shall act as President, as in the case of the death or other constitutional disability of the President. The person having the greatest number of votes as Vice-President, shall be the Vice-President, if such number be a majority of the whole number of Electors appointed, and if no person have a majority, then from the two highest numbers on the list, the Senate shall choose the Vice-President; a quorum for the purpose shall consist of two-thirds of the whole number of Senators, and a majority of the whole number shall be necessary to a choice. But no person constitutionally ineligible to the office of President shall be eligible to that of Vice-President of the United States.
Passed by Congress December 9, 1803. Ratified July 27, 1804.

13. Neither slavery nor involuntary servitude, except as a punishment for crime whereof the party shall have been duly convicted, shall exist within the United States, or any place subject to their jurisdiction.
Passed by Congress January 31, 1865. Ratified December 6, 1865.

14. Section 1.
All persons born or naturalized in the United States, and subject to the jurisdiction thereof, are citizens of the United States and of the State wherein they reside. No State shall

make or enforce any law which shall abridge the privileges or immunities of citizens of the United States; nor shall any State deprive any person of life, liberty, or property, without due process of law; nor deny to any person within its jurisdiction the equal protection of the laws.

Section 2.

Representatives shall be apportioned among the several States according to their respective numbers, counting the whole number of persons in each State, excluding Indians not taxed. But when the right to vote at any election for the choice of electors for President and Vice President of the United States, Representatives in Congress, the Executive and Judicial officers of a State, or the members of the Legislature thereof, is denied to any of the male inhabitants of such State, being twenty-one years of age, and citizens of the United States, or in any way abridged, except for participation in rebellion, or other crime, the basis of representation therein shall be reduced in the proportion which the number of such male citizens shall bear to the whole number of male citizens twenty-one years of age in such State.

Section 3.

No person shall be a Senator or Representative in Congress, or elector of President and Vice President, or hold any office, civil or military, under the United States, or under any State, who, having previously taken an oath, as a member of Congress, or as an officer of the United States, or as a member of any State legislature, or as an executive or judicial officer of any State, to support the Constitution of the United States, shall have engaged in insurrection or rebellion against the same, or given aid or comfort to the enemies thereof. But Congress may by a vote of two-thirds of each House, remove such disability.

Section 4.

The validity of the public debt of the United States, authorized by law, including debts incurred for payment of pensions and bounties for services in suppressing insurrection or rebellion, shall not be questioned. But neither the United States nor any State shall assume or pay any debt or obligation incurred in aid of insurrection or rebellion against the United States, or any claim for the loss or emancipation of any slave; but all such debts, obligations and claims shall be held illegal and void.

Section 5.

The Congress shall have power to enforce, by appropriate legislation, the provisions of this article.
Passed by Congress June 13, 1866. Ratified July 9, 1868.

15. Section 1.

The right of citizens of the United States to vote shall not be denied or abridged by the United States or by any State on account of race, color, or previous condition of servitude.

*The Liberty Bell in 1980,
hanging in Independence
National Historical Park,
Philadelphia.*

Section 2.

The Congress shall have power to enforce this article by appropriate legislation.

Passed by Congress February 26, 1869. Ratified February 3, 1870.

16. The Congress shall have power to lay and collect taxes on incomes, from whatever source derived, without apportionment among the several States and without regard to any census or enumeration.

Passed by Congress July 2, 1909. Ratified February 3, 1913.

17. The Senate of the United States shall be composed of two senators from each State, elected by the people thereof, for six years; and each Senator shall have one vote. The electors in each State shall have the qualifications requisite for electors of the most numerous branch of the State legislature.

When vacancies happen in the representation of any State in the Senate, the executive authority of such State shall issue writs of election to fill such vacancies: Provided, That the legislature of any State may empower the executive thereof to make temporary appointments until the people fill the vacancies by election as the legislature may direct.

This amendment shall not be so construed as to affect the election or term of any senator chosen before it becomes valid as part of the Constitution.

Passed by Congress May 13, 1912. Ratified April 8, 1913.

18. After one year from the ratification of this article, the manufacture, sale, or transportation of intoxicating liquors within, the importation thereof into, or the exportation thereof from the United States and all territory subject to the jurisdiction thereof for beverage purposes is hereby prohibited.

The Congress and the several States shall have concurrent power to enforce this article by appropriate legislation.

In 1751, to mark the 50th anniversary of Pennsylvania's founding, Philadelphia commissioned a bell for the State House (later Independence Hall) from Whitechapel Foundry in England. Inscribed on it was to be a line from Leviticus 25:10: "Proclaim Liberty throughout all the land unto all the inhabitants thereof," as well as "By Order of the assembly of the Province of Pensylvania for the State House in Philida." (Spelling had not yet been standardized. The state name appears similarly on the original Constitution.) The bell was delivered in 1752, but cracked from a stroke of the clapper while being raised to the steeple.

It was said there had been a flaw in the casting, or that the mix of metal was too brittle. John Pass and John Stow, two Philadelphia foundrymen, undertook to melt and recast the bell, adding more copper for flexibility. The bell, however, had a bad tone. Pass and Stow were so teased that they again melted and recast the bell. This proved better, and was raised to the steeple of the State House. Speaker of the Assembly, Isaac Norris, being not yet satisfied, commissioned a new bell from Whitechapel. But it had no better tone than the Pass and Stow bell, so it was placed in the cupola and rigged to a clock to ring the hours.

The Pass and Stow bell rang at the first public reading of the Declaration of Independence on July 8, 1776, but when the British occupied Philadelphia during the Revolutionary War it was removed, as were all bells, for fear the British would melt them for cannons. It was hidden under floorboards in a church in Allentown, PA. From 1778 it was rung on every July 4th until a crack rendered it unringable on Washington's birthday in 1846—a fitting metaphor for a nation split over slavery issues. After the Civil War, the Liberty Bell toured U.S. cities. It then hung in Independence Hall until the Liberty Bell Pavilion was erected for the Bicentennial.

This article shall be inoperative unless it shall have been ratified as an amendment to the Constitution by the legislatures of the several States, as provided in the Constitution, within seven years from the date of the submission hereof to the States by Congress.
Passed by Congress December 18, 1917. Ratified January 16, 1919. Altered by Amendment 21.

19. The right of citizens of the United States to vote shall not be denied or abridged by the United States or by any States on account of sex.

The Congress shall have power by appropriate legislation to enforce the provisions of this article.
Passed by Congress June 4, 1919. Ratified August 18, 1920.

20. Section 1.
The terms of the President and Vice-President shall end at noon on the twentieth day of January, and the terms of Senators and Representatives at noon on the third day of January, of the years in which such terms would have ended if this article had not been ratified; and the terms of their successors shall then begin.

Section 2.
The Congress shall assemble at least once in every year, and such meeting shall begin at noon on the third day of January, unless they shall by law appoint a different day.

Section 3.
If, at the time fixed for the beginning of the term of the President, the President-elect shall have died, the Vice-President-elect shall become President. If a President shall not have been chosen before the time fixed for the beginning of his term, or if the President-elect shall have failed to qualify, then the Vice-President-elect shall act as President until a President shall have qualified; and the Congress may by law provide for the case wherein neither a President-elect nor a Vice-President-elect shall have qualified, declaring who shall then act as President, or the manner in which one who is to act shall be selected, and such person shall act accordingly until a President or Vice-President shall have qualified.

Section 4.
The Congress may by law provide for the case of the death of any of the persons from whom the House of Representatives may choose a President whenever the right of choice shall have devolved upon them, and for the case of the death of any of the persons from whom the Senate may choose a Vice-President whenever the right of choice shall have devolved upon them.

Section 5.
Sections 1 and 2 shall take effect on the 15th day of October following the ratification of this article.

Section 6.
This article shall be inoperative unless it shall have been ratified as an amendment to the

A young visitor to the Liberty Bell at Independence Hall.

Constitution by the legislatures of three-fourths of the several States within seven years from the date of its submission.

Passed by Congress February 20, 1933. Ratified December 5, 1933.

21. Section 1.

The <u>eighteenth article of amendment</u> to the Constitution of the United States is hereby repealed.

Section 2.

The transportation or importation into any State, Territory, or possession of the United States for delivery or use therein of intoxicating liquors, in violation of the laws thereof, is hereby prohibited.

Section 3.

The article shall be inoperative unless it shall have been ratified as an amendment to the Constitution by conventions in the several States, as provided in the Constitution, within seven years from the date of the submission hereof to the States by the Congress.
Passed by Congress February 20, 1933. Ratified December 5, 1933.

22. Section 1.

No person shall be elected to the office of the President more than twice, and no person who has held the office of President, or acted as President for more than two years of a term to which some other person was elected President shall be elected to the office of the

President more than once. But this Article shall not apply to any person holding the office of President when this Article was proposed by the Congress, and shall not prevent any person who may be holding the office of President, or acting as President, during the term within which this Article becomes operative from holding the office of President or acting as President during the remainder of such term.

Section 2.
This article shall be inoperative unless it shall have been ratified as an amendment to the Constitution by the legislatures of three-fourths of the several States within seven years from the date of its submission to the States by the Congress.
Passed by Congress March 21, 1947. Ratified February 27, 1951.

23. Section 1.
The District constituting the seat of government of the United States shall appoint in such manner as the Congress may direct: A number of electors of President and Vice President equal to the whole number of Senators and Representatives in Congress to which the District would be entitled if it were a state, but in no event more than the least populous State; they shall be in addition to those appointed by the States, but they shall be considered, for the purposes of the election of President and Vice President, to be electors appointed by a State; and they shall meet in the district and perform such duties as provided by the twelfth article of amendment.

Section 2.
The Congress shall have power to enforce this article by appropriate legislation.
Passed by Congress June 16, 1960. Ratified March 29, 1961.

24. Section 1.
The right of citizens of the United States to vote in any primary or other election for President or Vice President, for electors for President or Vice President, or for Senator or Representative in Congress, shall not be denied or abridged by the United States or any State by reason of failure to pay any poll tax or other tax.

Section 2.
The Congress shall have power to enforce this article by appropriate legislation.
Passed by Congress August 27, 1962. Ratified January 23, 1964.

25. Section 1.
In case of the removal of the President from office or of his death or resignation, the Vice President shall become President.

Section 2.
Whenever there is a vacancy in the office of the Vice President, the President shall nominate a Vice President who shall take office upon confirmation by a majority vote of both Houses of Congress.

Section 3.

Whenever the President transmits to the President pro tempore of the Senate and the Speaker of the House of Representatives his written declaration that he is unable to discharge the powers and duties of his office, and until he transmits to them a written declaration to the contrary, such powers and duties shall be discharged by the Vice President as Acting President.

Section 4.

Whenever the Vice President and a majority of either the principal officers of the executive departments or of such other body as Congress may by law provide, transmit to the President pro tempore of the Senate and the Speaker of the House of Representatives their written declaration that the President is unable to discharge the powers and duties of his office, the Vice President shall immediately assume the powers and duties of the office as Acting President.

Thereafter, when the President transmits to the President pro tempore of the Senate and the Speaker of the House of Representatives his written declaration that no inability exists, he shall resume the powers and duties of his office unless the Vice President and a majority of either the principal officers of the executive department or of such other body as Congress may by law provide, transmit within four days to the President pro tempore of the Senate and the Speaker of the House of Representatives their written declaration that the President is unable to discharge the powers and duties of his office. Thereupon Congress shall decide the issue, assembling within forty-eight hours for that purpose if not in session. If the Congress, within twenty-one days after receipt of the latter written declaration, or, if Congress is not in session, within twenty-one days after Congress is required to assemble, determines by two-thirds vote of both Houses that the President is unable to discharge the powers and duties of his office, the Vice President shall continue to discharge the same as Acting President; otherwise, the President shall resume the powers and duties of his office. *Passed by Congress July 6, 1965. Ratified February 10, 1967.*

26. Section 1.

The right of citizens of the United States, who are eighteen years of age or older, to vote shall not be denied or abridged by the United States or by any State on account of age.

Section 2.

The Congress shall have power to enforce this article by appropriate legislation. *Passed by Congress March 23, 1971. Ratified June 30, 1971.*

27. No law, varying the compensation for the services of the Senators and Representatives, shall take effect, until an election of Representatives shall have intervened. *Originally proposed September 25, 1989. Ratified May 7, 1992.*

A view of Mt. Vernon, Washington's home.

FAREWELL ADDRESS (EXCERPTED)

George Washington, 1796

Friends and Fellow-citizens:

The period for a new election of a citizen to administer the executive government of the United States being not far distant, and the time actually arrived when your thoughts must be employed in designating the person who is to be clothed with that important trust, it appears to me proper. . . that I should now apprise you of the resolution I have formed, to decline being considered among the number of those out of whom a choice is to be made. . . .

The acceptance of, and continuance hitherto in, the office to which your suffrages have twice

called me have been a uniform sacrifice of inclination to the opinion of duty and to a deference for what appeared to be your desire. I constantly hoped that it would have been much earlier in my power . . . to return to that retirement from which I had been reluctantly drawn. The strength of my inclination to do this, previous to the last election, had even led to the preparation of an address to declare it to you; but mature reflection on the then perplexed and critical posture of our affairs with foreign nations, and the unanimous advice of persons entitled to my confidence, impelled me to abandon the idea. . . .

Washington had reluctantly agreed to continue on as President during the turbulent time after the Revolution, when the nation ran into trouble under the Articles of Confederation, before the Constitution was ratified. Although he himself wrote the first draft of his farewell, the final text was thoroughly edited and reworked by Alexander Hamilton. The new draft—barely recognizable from the original—pleased the President and was published in the American Daily Advertiser on September 19, 1796.

The full address runs to ten pages. Washington and Hamilton were anxious for the infant United States of America and its newly framed Constitutional government that both had worked so hard to bring into being. The document is wordy, but human and eerily prescient.

- *He stresses national union—to avoid regional divisiveness that might (and did) lead to situations like the Civil War.*

- *He warns against parties in government, and the misuse of lobbying or filibustering that can hamper or even cripple smooth government.*

- *He urges us to trust the system of checks and balances that has been set up by the Constitution, and allow it to work.*

- *He acknowledges human nature and stresses the importance of morality and religion.*

- *He recommends promoting education for all.*

- *He says to cherish public credit, and stay out of debt.*

- *He counsels fairness with all foreign nations. Do not play favorites with or hold onto a grudge against any other nation.*

- *He reveals isolationist leanings and suggests we stay out of others' conflicts and not meddle in other nations' affairs.*

- *He cautions that we not calculate or depend on favors from other nations.*

And he closes:

Though, in reviewing the incidents of my administration, I am unconscious of intentional error, I am nevertheless too sensible of my defects not to think it probable that I may have committed many errors. Whatever they may be, I fervently beseech the Almighty to avert or mitigate the evils to which they may tend. I shall also carry with me the hope that my country will never cease to view them with indulgence; and that, after forty five years of my life dedicated to its service with an upright zeal, the faults of incompetent abilities will be consigned to oblivion, as myself must soon be to the mansions of rest. . . .

Relying on its kindness in this as in other things, and actuated by that fervent love towards it, which is so natural to a man who views in it the native soil of himself and his progenitors for several generations, I anticipate with pleasing expectation that retreat in which I promise myself to realize, without alloy, the sweet enjoyment of partaking, in the midst of my fellow-citizens, the benign influence of good laws under a free government, the ever-favorite object of my heart, and the happy reward, as I trust, of our mutual cares, labors, and dangers.

GOD OF OUR FATHERS

Trumpets

1 God of our fa - thers, whose al - might - y
2 Thy love di - vine hath led us in the
3 From war's a - larms, from dead - ly pes - ti -
4 Re - fresh thy peo - ple on their toil - some

hand   leads forth in beau - ty   all the star - ry   band
past,   in this free land by   thee our lot is   cast;
lence,   be thy strong arm our   ev - er sure de - fense;
way,   lead us from night to   nev - er - end - ing   day;

of shin - ing worlds in splen - dor through the skies,
be thou our ru - ler, guard - ian, guide, and stay,
thy true re - li - gion in our hearts in - crease,
fill all our lives with love and grace di - vine,

our grate - ful songs be - fore thy throne a - rise.
thy word our law, thy paths our cho - sen way.
thy boun - teous good - ness nour - ish us in peace.
and glo - ry, laud, and praise be ev - er thine.

Mt. Rushmore.

Words: Daniel Crane Roberts (1841-1907)
Music: *National Hymn*, George William Warren (1828-1902)

PART III

FREEDOM
TESTED

Covered wagons pass Eagle Rock. To Americans at the beginning of the 19th century, the future seemed as vast and untrammeled as the western territories of the country—wide open and there for them to fulfill destiny's promise.

MANIFEST DESTINY

John L. O'Sullivan, 1839

The American people having derived their origin from many other nations, and the Declaration of National Independence being entirely based on the great principle of human equality, these facts demonstrate at once our disconnected position as regards any other nation; that we have, in reality, but little connection with the past history of any of them, and still less with all antiquity, its glories, or its crimes. On the contrary, our national birth was the beginning of a new history, the formation and progress of an untried political system, which separates us from the past and connects us with the future only; and so far as regards the entire development of the natural rights of man, in moral, political, and national life, we may confidently assume that our country is destined to be the great nation of futurity.

It is so destined, because the principle upon which a nation is organized fixes its destiny, and that of equality is perfect, is universal. It presides in all the operations of the physical world, and it is also the conscious law of the soul—the self-evident dictates of morality, which accurately defines the duty of man to man, and consequently man's rights as man. Besides, the truthful annals of any nation furnish abundant evidence, that its happiness, its greatness, its duration, were always proportionate to the democratic equality in its system of government. . . .

What friend of human liberty, civilization, and refinement, can cast his view over the past history of the monarchies and aristocracies of antiquity, and not deplore that they ever existed? What philanthropist can contemplate the oppressions, the cruelties, and injustice inflicted by them on the masses of mankind, and not turn with moral horror from the retrospect?

America is destined for better deeds. It is our unparalleled glory that we have no reminiscences of battle fields, but in defence of humanity, of the oppressed of all nations, of the rights of conscience, the rights of personal enfranchisement. Our annals describe no scenes of horrid carnage, where men were led on by hundreds of thousands to slay one another, dupes and victims to emperors, kings, nobles, demons in the human form called heroes. We have had patriots to defend our homes, our liberties, but no aspirants to crowns or thrones; nor have the American people ever suffered themselves to be led on by wicked ambition to depopulate the land, to spread desolation far and wide, that a human being might be placed on a seat of supremacy.

We have no interest in the scenes of antiquity, only as lessons of avoidance of nearly all their examples. The expansive future is our arena, and for our history. We are entering on its untrodden space, with the truths of God in our minds, beneficent objects in our hearts, and with a clear conscience unsullied by the past. We are the nation of human progress, and who will, what can, set limits to our onward march? Providence is with us, and no earthly power can. We point to the everlasting truth on the first page of our national declaration, and we proclaim to the millions of other lands, that "the gates of hell"—the powers of aristocracy and monarchy—"shall not prevail against it."

The far-reaching, the boundless future will be the era of American greatness. In its magnificent domain of space and time, the nation of many nations is destined to manifest to mankind the excellence of divine principles; to establish on earth the noblest temple ever dedicated to the worship of the Most High—the Sacred and the True. Its floor shall be a hemisphere—its roof the firmament of the star-studded heavens, and its congregation an Union of many Republics, comprising hundreds of happy millions, calling, owning no man master, but governed by God's natural and moral law of equality, the law of brotherhood—of "peace and good will amongst men."

Yes, we are the nation of progress, of individual freedom, of universal enfranchisement. Equality of rights is the cynosure of our union of States, the grand exemplar of the correlative equality of individuals; and while truth sheds its effulgence, we cannot retrograde, without dissolving the one and subverting the other. We must onward to the fulfilment of our mission —to the entire development of the principle of our organization—freedom of conscience, freedom of person, freedom of trade and business pursuits, universality of freedom and equality. This is our high destiny, and in nature's eternal, inevitable decree of cause and effect we must accomplish it. All this will be our future history, to establish on earth the moral dignity and salvation of man—the immutable truth and beneficence of God. For this blessed mission to the nations of the world, which are shut out from the life-giving light of truth, has America been chosen; and her high example shall smite unto death the tyranny of kings, hierarchs, and oligarchs, and carry the glad tidings of peace and good will where myriads now endure an existence scarcely more enviable than that of beasts of the field. Who, then, can doubt that our country is destined to be *the great nation* of futurity?

THE SENECA FALLS DECLARATION

Elizabeth Cady Stanton, July 19, 1848

1. Declaration of Sentiments

When, in the course of human events, it becomes necessary for one portion of the family of man to assume among the people of the earth a position different from that which they have hitherto occupied, but one to which the laws of nature and of nature's God entitle them, a decent respect to the opinions of mankind requires that they should declare the causes that impel them to such a course.

We hold these truths to be self-evident: that all men and women are created equal; that they are endowed by their Creator with certain inalienable rights; that among these are life, liberty, and the pursuit of happiness; that to secure these rights governments are instituted, deriving their just powers from the consent of the governed. Whenever any form of government becomes destructive of these ends, it is the right of those who suffer from it to refuse allegiance to it, and to insist upon the institution of a new government, laying its foundation on such principles, and organizing its powers in such form, as to them shall seem most likely to effect their safety and happiness. Prudence, indeed, will dictate that governments long established should not be changed for light and transient causes; and accordingly all experience hath shown that mankind are more disposed to suffer while evils are sufferable, than to right themselves by abolishing the forms to which they are accustomed. But when a long train of abuses and usurpations, pursuing invariably the same object, evinces a design to reduce them under absolute despotism, it is their duty to throw off such government, and to provide new guards for their future security. Such has been the patient sufferance of the women under this government, and such

Engraving by H.B. Hall of the American reformer and suffragette Elizabeth Cady Stanton (1815-1902). Along with Lucretia Mott and Susan B. Anthony, she was an early crusader and spokesperson for women's rights and an editor of the feminist magazine Revolution.

is now the necessity which constrains them to demand the equal station to which they are entitled. The history of mankind is a history of repeated injuries and usurpations on the part of man toward woman, having in direct object the establishment of an absolute tyranny over her. To prove this, let facts be submitted to a candid world.

He has never permitted her to exercise her inalienable right to the elective franchise.

He has compelled her to submit to laws, in the formation of which she had no voice.

He has withheld from her rights which are given to the most ignorant and degraded men—both natives and foreigners.

Having deprived her of this first right of a citizen, the elective franchise, thereby leaving her without representation in the halls of legislation, he has oppressed her on all sides.

He has made her, if married, in the eye of the law, civilly dead. He has taken from her all right in property, even to the wages she earns.

He has made her, morally, an irresponsible being, as she can commit many crimes with impunity, provided they be done in the presence of her husband.

In the covenant of marriage, she is compelled to promise obedience to her husband, he becoming, to all intents and purposes, her master—the law giving him power to deprive her of her liberty and to administer chastisement.

He has so framed the laws of divorce, as to what shall be the proper causes, and in case of separation, to whom the guardianship of the children shall be given, as to be wholly regardless of the happiness of women—the law, in all cases, going upon a false supposition of the supremacy of man, and giving all power into his hands.

After depriving her of all rights as a married woman, if single, and the owner of property, he has taxed her to support a government which recognizes her only when her property can be made profitable to it.

He has monopolized nearly all the profitable employments, and from those she is permitted to follow, she receives but a scanty remuneration. He closes against her all the avenues to wealth and distinction which he considers most honorable to himself. As a teacher of theology, medicine, or law, she is not known.

He has denied her the facilities for obtaining a thorough education, all colleges being closed against her.

He allows her in Church, as well as State, but a subordinate position, claiming Apostolic authority for her exclusion from the ministry, and, with some exceptions, from any public participation in the affairs of the Church.

He has created a false public sentiment by giving to the world a different code of morals for men and women, by which moral delinquencies which exclude women from society, are not only tolerated, but deemed of little account in man.

He has usurped the prerogative of Jehovah himself, claiming it as his right to assign for her a sphere of action, when that belongs to her conscience and to her God.

He has endeavored, in every way that he could, to destroy her confidence in her own powers, to lessen her self-respect and to make her willing to lead a dependent and abject life.

Now, in view of this entire disfranchisement of one-half the people of this country, their social and religious degradation—in view of the unjust laws above mentioned, and because women do feel themselves aggrieved, oppressed, and fraudulently deprived of their most sacred rights, we insist that they have immediate admission to all the rights and privileges which belong to them as citizens of the United States.

In entering upon the great work before us. we anticipate no small amount of misconception, misrepresentation, and ridicule; but we shall use every instrumentality within our power to effect our object. We shall employ agents, circulate tracts, petition the State and National legislatures, and endeavor to enlist the pulpit and the press in our behalf. We hope this Convention will be followed by a series of Conventions embracing every part of the country.

Within two years of Elizabeth Cady Stanton's declaration, early suffragettes devised a fashion to free themselves from the constraints of current women's wear. They substituted bloomers topped by a shorter skirt for the long skirts, hoops, and petticoats then worn. It caused The Bloomerism Scandal. Here, a cartoon by Leech depicts how masculine women would become. Smoking and reading newspapers were considered inappropriate activities for women in that era.

2. Resolutions

WHEREAS, The great precept of nature is conceded to be, that "man shall pursue his own true and substantial happiness." Blackstone in his Commentaries remarks, that this law of Nature being coeval with mankind, and dictated by God himself, is of course superior in obligation to any other. It is binding over all the globe, in all countries and at all times; no human laws are of any validity if contrary to this, and such of them as are valid, derive all their force. and all their validity, and all their authority, mediately and immediately, from this original; therefore,

Resolved, That such laws as conflict, in any way with the true and substantial happiness of woman, are contrary to the great precept of nature and of no validity, for this is "superior in obligation to any other."

Resolved, That all laws which prevent woman from occupying such a station in society as her conscience shall dictate, or which place her in a position inferior to that of man, are contrary to the great precept of nature, and therefore of no force or authority.

Resolved, That woman is man's equal—was intended to be so by the Creator, and the highest good of the race demands that she should be recognized as such.

Resolved, That the women of this country ought to be enlightened in regard to the laws under which they live, that they may no longer publish their degradation by declaring themselves satisfied with their present position, nor their ignorance, by asserting that they have all the rights they want.

Resolved, That inasmuch as man, while claiming for himself intellectual superiority, does accord to woman moral superiority, it is pre-eminently his duty to encourage her to speak and teach, as she has an opportunity, in all religious assemblies.

Resolved, That the same amount of virtue, delicacy, and refinement of behavior that is required of woman in the social state, should also be required of man, and the same transgressions should be visited with equal severity on both man and woman.

Resolved, That the objection of indelicacy and impropriety, which is so often brought against woman when she addresses a public audience, comes with a very ill-grace from those who encourage, by their attendance, her appearance on the stage, in the concert, or in feats of the circus.

Resolved, That woman has too long rested satisfied in the circumscribed limits which corrupt customs and a perverted application of the Scriptures have marked out for her, and that it is time she should move in the enlarged sphere which her great Creator has assigned her.

Resolved, That it is the duty of the women of this country to secure to themselves their sacred right to the elective franchise.

Resolved, That the equality of human rights results necessarily from the fact of the identity of the race in capabilities and responsibilities.

Resolved therefore, That, being invested by the creator with the same capabilities, and the same consciousness of responsibility for their exercise, it is demonstrably the right and duty of woman, equally with man, to promote every righteous cause by every righteous means; and especially in regard to the great subjects of morals and religion, it is self-evidently her right to participate with her brother in teaching them, both in private and in public, by writing and by speaking, by any instrumentalities proper to be used, and in any assemblies proper to be held; and this being a self evident truth growing out of the divinely implanted principles of human nature, any custom or authority adverse to it, whether modern or wearing the hoary sanction of antiquity, is to be regarded as a self- evident falsehood, and at war with mankind.

Resolved, That the speedy success of our cause depends upon the zealous and untiring efforts of both men and women, for the overthrow of the monopoly of the pulpit, and for the securing to women an equal participation with men in the various trades, professions, and commerce.

"A House Divided"

Abraham Lincoln, June 16, 1858

Speech Made As Republican Nominee For Senator, Springfield, Illinois

Mr. PRESIDENT and Gentlemen of the Convention, if we could first know *where* we are, and *whither* we are tending, we could then better judge *what* to do, and *how* to do it.

We are now far into the *fifth* year, since a policy was initiated, with the *avowed* object, and *confident* promise, of putting an end to slavery agitation.

Under the operation of that policy, that agitation has not only, *not ceased,* but has *constantly augmented.*

In *my* opinion, it *will* not cease, until a *crisis* shall have been reached, and passed.

"A house divided against itself cannot stand."

I believe this government cannot endure, permanently half *slave* and half *free.*

I do not expect the Union to be *dissolved—I* do not expect the house to *fall—but* I *do* expect it will cease to be divided.

It will become *all* one thing, or *all* the other.

Either the *opponents* of slavery, will arrest the further spread of it, and place it where the public mind shall rest in the belief that it is in course of ultimate extinction; or its *advocates* will push it forward, till it shall become alike lawful in *all* the States, *old* as well as *new—North* as well as *South.*

Have we no *tendency* to the latter condition?

Let any one who doubts, carefully contemplate that now almost complete legal combination—piece of *machinery* so to speak—compounded of the Nebraska doctrine, and the Dred Scott decision. Let him consider not only *what work* the machinery is adapted to do, and *how well*

The front page of Frank Leslie's Illustrated Newspaper, covering the Dred Scott case in 1857. The Supreme Court ruled that slaves entering a non-slave state could not therefore gain their freedom. The decision increased anti-slavery feeling in the North, leading to the American Civil War.

adapted; but also, let him study the *history* of its construction, and trace, if he can, or rather *fail,* if he can, to trace the evidences of design, and concert of action, among its chief bosses, from the beginning.

The new year of 1854 found slavery excluded from more than half the States by State Constitutions, and from most of the national territory by Congressional prohibition.

Four days later, commenced the struggle, which ended in repealing that Congressional prohibition.

This opened all the national territory to slavery; and was the first point gained.

But, so far, *Congress* only, had acted; and an *indorsement* by the people, *real* or apparent, was indispensable, to *save* the point already gained, and give chance for more.

This necessity had not been overlooked; but had been provided for, as

An old farmstead site. In the mid-1800s, as people moved to settle new territories, issues over "free states" and whether a slave remained a slave if the master moved to a free territory are at the heart of the Dred Scott case and Lincoln's speech.

well as might be, in the notable argument of *"squatter sovereignty,"* otherwise called *"sacred right of self government,"* which latter phrase, though expressive of the only rightful basis of any government, was so perverted in this attempted use of it as to amount to just this: That if any *one* man, choose to enslave *another*, no *third* man shall be allowed to object.

That argument was incorporated into the Nebraska bill itself, in the language which follows: *"It being the true intent and meaning of this act not to legislate slavery into any Territory or state, not exclude it therefrom; but to leave the people thereof perfectly free to form and regulate their domestic institutions in their own way, subject only to the Constitution of the United States."*

Then opened the roar of loose declamation in favor of "Squatter Sovereignty," and "Sacred right of self government."

"But," said opposition members, "let us be more *specific—let us amend* the bill so as to expressly declare that the people of the territory *may* exclude slavery." "Not we," said the friends of the measure; and down they voted the amendment.

While the Nebraska bill was passing through congress, a *law case,* involving the question of a negroe's freedom, by reason of his owner having voluntarily taken him first into a free state and then a territory covered by the congressional prohibition, and held him as a slave, for a long time in each, was passing through the U.S. Circuit Court for the District of Missouri; and both Nebraska bill and law suit were brought to a decision in the same month of May, 1854. The negroe's name was "Dred Scott," which name now designates the decision finally made in the case.

Before the *then* next Presidential election, the law case came *to,* and was argued *in* the Supreme Court of the United States; but the decision of it was deferred until *after* the election. Still, *before* the election, Senator Trumbull, on the floor of the Senate, requests the leading advocate of the Nebraska bill to state *his opinion* whether the people of a territory can constitutionally exclude slavery from their limits; and the latter answers, "That is a question for the Supreme Court."

The election came. Mr. Buchanan was elected, and the *indorsement,* such as it was, secured. That was the *second* point gained. The indorsement, however, fell short of a clear popular majority by nearly four hundred thousand votes, and so, perhaps, was not overwhelmingly reliable and satisfactory.

The *outgoing* President, in his last annual message, as impressively as possible *echoed back* upon the people the *weight* and *authority* of the indorsement.

The Supreme Court met again; *did not* announce their decision, but ordered a re-argument.

The Presidential inauguration came, and still no decision of the court; but the *incoming* President, in his inaugural address, fervently exhorted the people to abide by the forthcoming decision, *whatever it might be.*

Then, in a few days, came the decision.

The reputed author of the Nebraska bill finds an early occasion to make a speech at this capitol indorsing the Dred Scott Decision, and vehemently denouncing all opposition to it.

The new President, too, seizes the early occasion of the Silliman letter to *indorse* and strongly *construe* that decision, and to express his *astonishment* that any different view had ever been entertained.

At length a squabble springs up between the President and the author of the Nebraska bill, on the *mere* question of *fact,* whether the Lecompton constitution was or was not, in any just sense, made by the people of Kansas; and in that squabble the latter declares that all he wants is a fair vote for the people, and that he *cares* not whether slavery be voted *down* or voted up. I do not understand his declaration that he cares not whether slavery be voted down or voted up, to be intended by him other than as an *apt definition* of the *policy* he would impress upon the public mind—the *principle* for which he declares he has suffered much, and is ready to suffer to the end.

And well may he cling to that principle. If he has any parental feeling, well may he cling to it. That principle, is the only *shred* left of his original Nebraska doctrine. Under the Dred Scott decision, "squatter sovereignty" squatted out of existence, tumbled down like temporary scaffolding—like the mould at the foundry served through one blast and fell back into loose sand— helped to carry an election, and then was kicked to the winds. His late *joint* struggle with the Republicans, against the Lecompton Constitution, involves nothing of the original Nebraska doctrine. That struggle was made on a point, the right of a people to make their own Constitution, upon which he and the Republicans have never differed.

The several points of the Dred Scott decision, in connection with Senator Douglas' "care not" policy, constitute the piece of machinery, in its *present* state of advancement. This was the third point gained.

The *working* points of that machinery are:

First, that no negro slave, imported as such from Africa, and no descendant of such slave can ever be a *citizen* of any State, in the sense of that term as used in the Constitution of the United States.

This point is made in order to deprive the negro, in every possible event, of the benefit of this provision of the United States Constitution, which declares that-

"The citizens of each State shall be entitled to all privileges and immunities of citizens in the several States."

Secondly, that "subject to the Constitution of the United States," neither *Congress* nor a *Territorial Legislature* can exclude slavery from any United States territory.

This point is made in order that individual men may *fill up* the territories with slaves, without danger of losing them as property, and thus to enhance the chances of *permanency* to the institution through all the future.

Thirdly, that whether the holding a negro in actual slavery in a free State, makes him free, as against the holder, the United States courts will not decide, but will leave to be decided by the courts of any slave State the negro may be forced into by the master.

This point is made, not to be pressed *immediately;* but, if acquiesced in for a while, and apparently *indorsed* by the people at an election, *then* to sustain the logical conclusion that what Dred Scott's master might lawfully do with Dred Scott, in the free State of Illinois, every other master may lawfully do with any other *one*, or one *thousand* slaves, in Illinois, or in any other free State.

Auxiliary to all this, and working hand in hand with it, the Nebraska doctrine, or what is left of it, is to *educate* and *mould* public opinion, at least *Northern* public opinion, to not *care* whether slavery is voted *down* or voted *up*.

This shows exactly where we now *are*; and *partially* also, whither we are tending.

It will throw additional light on the latter, to go back, and run the mind over the string of historical facts already stated. Several things will *now* appear less *dark* and *mysterious* than they did *when* they were transpiring. The people were to be left "perfectly free" "subject only to the Constitution." What the *Constitution* had to do with it, outsiders could not *then* see. Plainly

The house would divide—that is, the United States split, over bitter disagreements about slavery.
A painting of Antietam, Maryland, September 17, 1862.

enough *now*, it was an exactly fitted *niche*, for the Dred Scott decision to afterwards come in, and declare the *perfect freedom* of the people, to be just no freedom at all.

Why was the amendment, expressly declaring the right of the people to exclude slavery, voted down? Plainly enough *now*, the adoption of it, would have spoiled the niche for the Dred Scott decision.

Why was the court decision held up? Why, even a Senator's individual opinion withheld, till *after* the Presidential election? Plainly enough *now*, the speaking out *then* would have damaged the *"perfectly free"* argument upon which the election was to be carried.

Why the *outgoing* President's felicitation on the indorsement? Why the delay of a reargument? Why the incoming President's *advance* exhortation in favor of the decision?

These things *look* like the cautious *patting* and *petting* a spirited horse, preparatory to mounting him, when it is dreaded that he may give the rider a fall.

Antietam as it is today. Notice the same three-arched stone bridge that appears in the artist's rendering on page 97.

And why the hasty after indorsements of the decision by the President and others?

We can not absolutely *know* that all these exact adaptations are the result of preconcert. But when we see a lot of framed timbers, different portions of which we know have been gotten out at different times and places and by different workmen—Stephen, Franklin, Roger and James, for instance—and when we see these timbers joined together, and see they exactly make the frame of a house or a mill, all the tenons and mortices exactly fitting, and all the lengths and proportions of the different pieces exactly adapted to their respective places, and not a piece too many or too few—not omitting even scaffolding—or, if a single piece be lacking, we can see the place in the frame exactly fitted and prepared to yet bring such piece in—in *such* a case, we find it impossible to not *believe* that Stephen and Franklin and Roger and James all understood one another from the beginning, and all worked upon a common *plan* or *draft* drawn up before the first lick was struck.

It should not be overlooked that, by the Nebraska bill, the people of a *State* as well as *Territory*, were to be left *"perfectly free"* *"subject only to the Constitution."*

Why mention a *State?* They were legislating for *territories,* and not *for or about* States. Certainly the people of a State *are* and *ought to be* subject to the Constitution of the United States; but why is mention of this *lugged* into this merely *territorial* law? Why are the people of a *territory* and the people of a *state* therein *lumped* together, and their relation to the Constitution therein treated as being *precisely* the same?

While the opinion of *the Court,* by Chief Justice Taney, in the Dred Scott case, and the separate opinions of all the concurring Judges, expressly declare that the Constitution of the United States neither permits Congress nor a Territorial legislature to exclude slavery from any United States territory, they all *omit* to declare whether or not the same Constitution permits a *state,* or the people of a State, to exclude it.

Possibly, this was a mere *omission;* but who can be *quite* sure, if McLean or Curtis had sought to get into the opinion a declaration of unlimited power in the people of a *state* to exclude slavery from their limits, just as Chase and Macy sought to get such declaration, in behalf of the people of a territory, into the Nebraska bill—I ask, who can be quite *sure* that it would not have been voted down, in the one case, as it had been in the other.

The nearest approach to the point of declaring the power of a State over slavery, is made by Judge Nelson. He approaches it more than once, using the precise idea, and *almost* the language too, of the Nebraska act. On one occasion his exact language is, "except in cases where the power is restrained by the Constitution of the United States, the law of the State is supreme over the subject of slavery within its jurisdiction."

In what *cases* the power of the *states is so* restrained by the U.S. Constitution, is left an *open* question, precisely as the same question, as to the restraint on the power of the *territories* was left open in the Nebraska act. Put *that* and *that* together, and we have another nice little niche, which we may, ere long, see filled with another Supreme Court decision, declaring that the Constitution of the United States does not permit a *state* to exclude slavery from its limits.

And this may especially be expected if the doctrine of "care not whether slavery be voted *down* or voted up," shall gain upon the public mind sufficiently to give promise that such a decision can be maintained when made.

Such a decision is all that slavery now lacks of being alike lawful in all the States.

Welcome or unwelcome, such decision *is* probably coming, and will soon be upon us, unless the power of the present political dynasty shall be met and overthrown.

We shall *lie down* pleasantly dreaming that the people of *Missouri* are on the verge of making their State *free,* and we shall *awake* to the *reality,* instead, that the *Supreme* Court has made *Illinois* a *slave* State.

To meet and overthrow the power of that dynasty, is the work now before all those who would prevent that consummation.

That is *what* we have to do.

But *how* can we best do it?

There are those who denounce *us openly* to their *own* friends, and yet whisper us *softly*, that *Senator Douglas* is the *aptest* instrument there is, with which to effect that object. *They* do *not* tell us, nor has *he* told us, that he *wishes* any such object to be effected. They wish us to *infer* all, from the facts, that he now has a little quarrel with the present head of the dynasty; and that he has regularly voted with us, on a single point, upon which, he and we, have never differed.

They remind us that *he is* a very *great man,* and that the largest of us are very small ones. Let this be granted. But "a *living dog is* better than a *dead lion."* Judge Douglas, if not a *dead* lion *for this work,* is at least a *caged* and *toothless* one. How can he oppose the advances of slavery? He don't *care* anything about it. His avowed *mission is impressing* the "public heart" to *care* nothing about it.

A leading Douglas Democratic newspaper thinks Douglas' superior talent will be needed to resist the revival of the African slave trade.

Does Douglas believe an effort to revive that trade is approaching? He has not said so. Does he *really* think so? But if it is, how can he resist it? For years he has labored to prove of white men to take negro slaves into the new territories. Can he possibly show that it is *less* a sacred right to *buy* them where they can be bought cheapest? And unquestionably they can be bought *cheaper in Africa* than in *Virginia.*

He has done all in his power to reduce the whole question of slavery to one of a mere *right of property,* and as such, how can *he* oppose the foreign slave trade—how can he refuse that trade in that "property" shall be "perfectly free"—unless he does it as a *protection* to the home production? And as the home *producers* will probably not *ask* the protection, he will be wholly without aground of opposition.

Senator Douglas holds, we know, that a man may rightfully be *wiser to-day* than he was *yesterday—that* he may rightfully *change* when he finds himself wrong.

But, can we for that reason, run ahead, and *infer* that he *will* make any particular change, of which he, himself, has given no intimation? Can we *safely* base *our* action upon any such *vague* inference?

Now, as ever, I wish to not *misrepresent* Judge Douglas' *position,* question his *motives,* or do ought that can be personally offensive to him.

Whenever, *if ever,* he and we can come together on *principle* so that *our great cause* may have assistance from *his great ability,* I hope to have interposed no adventitious obstacle.

But clearly, he is not *now* with us—he does not *pretend* to be—he does not *promise* to *ever* be.

The site of the Battle of Chattanooga, "Gateway to the Lower South," fought November 23–25, 1863. Lincoln said that, " . . . taking Chattanooga is as important as taking Richmond."

Our cause, then, must be intrusted to, and conducted by its own undoubted friends—those whose hands are free, whose hearts are in the work—who *do care* for the result.

Two years ago the Republicans of the nation mustered over thirteen hundred thousand strong.

We did this under the single impulse of resistance to a common danger, with every external circumstance against us.

Of *strange, discordant,* and even, *hostile* elements, we gathered from the four winds, and *formed* and fought the battle through, under the constant hot fire of a disciplined, proud, and pampered enemy.

Did we brave all *then,* to *falter* now? Now—when that same enemy is *wavering,* dissevered and belligerent?

The result is not doubtful. We shall not fail—if we stand firm, we shall not fail.

Wise councils may *accelerate* or *mistakes delay* it, but, sooner or later the victory is *sure* to come.

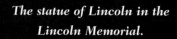

The statue of Lincoln in the
Lincoln Memorial.

EMANCIPATION PROCLAMATION

President Abraham Lincoln, January 1, 1863

By the President of the United States of America: A Proclamation.

Whereas, on the twenty second day of September, in the year of our Lord one thousand eight hundred and sixty two, a proclamation was issued by the President of the United States, containing, among other things, the following, to wit:

"That on the first day of January, in the year of our Lord one thousand eight hundred and sixty-three, all persons held as slaves within any State or designated part of a State, the people whereof shall then be in rebellion against the United States, shall be then, thenceforward, and forever free; and the Executive Government of the United States, including the military and naval authority thereof, will recognize and maintain the freedom of such persons, and will do no act or acts to repress such persons, or any of them, in any efforts they may make for their actual freedom.

"That the Executive will, on the first day of January aforesaid, by proclamation, designate the States and parts of States, if any, in which the people thereof, respectively, shall then be in rebellion against the United States; and the fact that any State, or the people thereof, shall on that day be, in good faith, represented in the Congress of the United States by members chosen thereto at elections wherein a majority of the qualified voters of such State shall have participated, shall, in the absence of strong countervailing testimony, be deemed conclusive evidence that such State, and the people thereof, are not then in rebellion against the United States."

Now, therefore I, Abraham Lincoln, President of the United States, by virtue of the power in me vested as Commander-in-Chief, of the Army and Navy of the United States in time of actual armed rebellion against authority and government of the United States, and as a fit and necessary war measure for suppressing said rebellion, do, on this first day of January, in the year of our Lord one thousand eight hundred and sixty three, and in accordance with my purpose so to do publicly proclaimed for the full period of one hundred days, from the day first above mentioned, order and designate as the States and parts of States wherein the people thereof respectively, are this day in rebellion against the United States, the following, towit:

Arkansas, Texas, Louisiana, (except the Parishes of St. Bernard, Plaquemines, Jefferson, St. Johns, St. Charles, St. James[,] Ascension, Assumption, Terrebonne, Lafourche, St. Mary, St. Martin, and Orleans, including the City of New-Orleans) Mississippi, Alabama, Florida, Georgia, South-Carolina, North-Carolina, and Virginia, (except the fortyeight counties designated as West Virginia, and also the counties of Berkley, Accomac, Northampton, Elizabeth-City, York, Princess Ann, and Norfolk, including the cities of Norfolk & Portsmouth []); and which excepted parts are, for the present, left precisely as if this proclamation were not issued.

And by virtue of the power, and for the purpose aforesaid, I do order and declare that all persons held as slaves within said designated States, and parts of States, are, and henceforward shall be free; and that the Executive government of the United States, including the military and naval authorities thereof, will recognize and maintain the freedom of said persons.

And I hereby enjoin upon the people so declared to be free to abstain from all violence, unless in necessary self-defence; and I recommend to them that, in all cases when allowed, they labor faithfully for reasonable wages.

And I further declare and make known, that such persons of suitable condition, will be received into the armed service of the United States to garrison forts, positions, stations, and other places, and to man vessels of all sorts in said service.

And upon this act, sincerely believed to be an act of justice, warranted by the Constitution, upon military necessity, I invoke the considerate judgment of mankind, and the gracious favor of Almighty God.

In witness whereof, I have hereunto set my hand and caused the seal of the United States to be affixed.

Done at the City of Washington, this first day of January, in the year of our Lord one thousand eight hundred and sixty three, and of the Independence of the United States of America the eighty-seventh.

By the President: ABRAHAM LINCOLN

WILLIAM H. SEWARD, Secretary of State.

The Gettysburg Address

President Abraham Lincoln, November 19, 1863

Address delivered at the dedication of the cemetery at Gettysburg

Four score and seven years ago our fathers brought forth on this continent, a new nation, conceived in Liberty, and dedicated to the proposition that all men are created equal.

Now we are engaged in a great civil war, testing whether that nation, or any nation so conceived and so dedicated, can long endure. We are met on a great battlefield of that war. We have come to dedicate a portion of that field, as a final resting place for those who here gave their lives that that nation might live. It is altogether fitting and proper that we should do this.

But, in a larger sense, we cannot dedicate—we cannot consecrate—we can not hallow—this ground. The brave men, living and dead, who struggled here, have consecrated it, far above our poor power to add or detract. The world will little note, nor long remember what we say here, but it can never forget what they did here. It is for us the living, rather, to be dedicated here to the unfinished work which they who fought here have thus far so nobly advanced. It is rather

An 1884 color illustration of a portion of the Battle of Gettysburg. The battle lasted from July 1–3, 1863, between Union forces led by Major General George G. Meade and Confederates led by General Robert E. Lee. It was a crucial point in the Civil War. Lee's defeat caused him to break off his planned invasion of the North.

A view of Gettysburg today.

for us to be here dedicated to the great task remaining before us—that from these honored dead we take increased devotion to that cause for which they gave the last full measure of devotion—that we here highly resolve that these dead shall not have died in vain—that this nation, under God, shall have a new birth of freedom—and that government of the people, by the people, for the people, shall not perish from the earth.

November 19, 1863. Abraham Lincoln.

"WHAT THE BLACK MAN WANTS"

Frederick Douglass, Boston, April 1865

At the Annual Meeting of the Massachusetts Anti-Slavery Society, Douglass delivered the follow-ing speech on the subject: The Equality of all men before the law. (Note that this was given with-in days of the close of the Civil War and the assassination of President Lincoln.)

I came here, as I come always to the meetings in New England, as a listener, and not as a speaker; and one of the reasons why I have not been more frequently to the meetings of this society, has been because of the disposition on the part of some of my friends to call me out upon the platform, even when they knew that there was some difference of opinion and of feeling between those who rightfully belong to this platform and myself; and for fear of being misconstrued, as desiring to interrupt or disturb the proceedings of these meetings, I have usu-ally kept away, and have thus been deprived of that educating influence, which I am always free to confess is of the highest order, descending from this platform. I have felt, since I have lived out West [Douglass means west of Boston, in Rochester, NY], that in going there I parted from a great deal that was valuable; and I feel, every time I come to these meetings, that I have lost a great deal by making my home west of Boston, west of Massachusetts; for, if anywhere in the country there is to be found the highest sense of justice, or the truest demands for my race, I look for it in the East, I look for it here. The ablest discussions of the whole question of our rights occur here, and to be deprived of the privilege of listening to those discussions is a great deprivation.

I do not know, from what has been said, that there is any difference of opinion as to the duty of abolitionists, at the present moment. How can we get up any difference at this point, or any point, where we are so united, so agreed? I went especially, however, with that word of Mr. Phillips, which is the criticism of Gen. Banks and Gen. Banks' policy. [Gen. Banks instituted a labor policy in Louisiana that was discriminatory of blacks, claiming that it was to help prepare them to better handle freedom. Wendell Phillips countered by saying, "If there is anything patent in the whole history of our thirty years' struggle, it is that the Negro no more needs to be prepared for liberty than the white man."] I hold that that policy is our chief danger at the pres-ent moment; that it practically enslaves the Negro, and makes the Proclamation [the Emancipation Proclamation] of 1863 a mockery and delusion. What is freedom? It is the right to choose one's own employment. Certainly it means that, if it means anything; and when any individual or combination of individuals undertakes to decide for any man when he shall work, where he shall work, at what he shall work, and for what he shall work, he or they practically reduce him to slavery. [Applause.] He is a slave. That I understand Gen. Banks to do—to determine for the so-called freedman, when, and where, and at what, and for how much he shall work, when he shall be punished, and by whom punished. It is absolute slavery. It defeats the beneficent intention of the Government, if it has beneficent intentions, in regards to the freedom of our people.

The former slave Frederick Douglass (1817–1895), circa 1850. After his escape he campaigned against slavery and for black civil rights. His autobiography has become a classic work of American literature.

I have had but one idea for the last three years to present to the American people, and the phraseology in which I clothe it is the old abolition phraseology. I am for the "immediate, unconditional, and universal" enfranchisement of the black man, in every State in the Union. [Loud applause.] Without this, his liberty is a mockery; without this, you might as well almost retain the old name of slavery for his condition; for in fact, if he is not the slave of the individual master, he is the slave of society, and holds his liberty as a privilege, not as a right. He is at the mercy of the mob, and has no means of protecting himself.

It may be objected, however, that this pressing of the Negro's right to suffrage is premature. Let us have slavery abolished, it may be said, let us have labor organized, and then, in the natural course of events, the right of suffrage will be extended to the Negro. I do not agree with this. The constitution of the human mind is such, that if it once disregards the conviction forced upon it by a revelation of truth, it requires the exercise of a higher power to produce the same conviction afterwards. The American people are now in tears. The Shenandoah has run blood—the best blood of the North. All around Richmond, the blood of New England and of the North has been shed—of your sons, your brothers and your fathers. We all feel, in the existence of this Rebellion, that judgments terrible, wide-spread, far-reaching, overwhelming, are abroad in the land; and we feel, in view of these judgments, just now, a disposition to learn righteousness. This is the hour. Our streets are in mourning, tears are falling at every fireside, and under the chastisement of this Rebellion we have almost come up to the point of conceding this great, this all-important right of suffrage. I fear that if we fail to do it now, if abolitionists fail to press it now, we may not see, for centuries to come, the same disposition that exists at this moment. [Applause.] Hence, I say, now is the time to press this right.

It may be asked, "Why do you want it? Some men have got along very well without it. Women have not this right." Shall we justify one wrong by another? This is the sufficient answer. Shall we at this moment justify the deprivation of the Negro of the right to vote, because some one else is deprived of that privilege? I hold that women, as well as men, have the right to vote [applause], and my heart and voice go with the movement to extend suffrage to woman; but that question rests upon another basis than which our right rests. We may be asked, I say, why we want it. I will tell you why we want it. We want it because it is our right, first of all. No class of men can, without insulting their own nature, be content with any deprivation of their rights. We want it again, as a means for educating our race. Men are so constituted that they derive their conviction of their own possibilities largely by the estimate formed of them by others. If nothing is expected of a people, that people will find it difficult to contradict that expectation. By depriving us of suffrage, you affirm our incapacity to form an intelligent judgment respecting public men and public measures; you declare before the world that we are unfit to exercise the elective franchise, and by this means lead us to undervalue ourselves, to put a low estimate upon ourselves, and to feel that we have no possibilities like other men. Again, I want the elective franchise, for one, as a colored man, because ours is a peculiar government, based upon a peculiar idea, and that idea is universal suffrage. If I were in a monarchial government, or an autocratic or aristocratic government, where the few bore rule and the many were subject, there would be no special stigma resting upon me, because I did not exercise the elective franchise. It would do me no great violence. Mingling with the mass I should partake of the strength of the mass; I should be supported by the mass, and I should have the same incentives to endeavor with the mass of my fellow-men; it would be no particular burden, no particular deprivation; but here where universal suffrage is the rule, where that is the fundamental idea of the Government, to rule us out is to make us an exception, to brand us with the stigma of inferiority, and to invite to our heads the missiles of those about us; therefore, I want the franchise for the black man.

Wendell Phillips (1811–1884), President of the Anti-Slavery Society between 1865-70. An abolitionist from 1837, he also promoted penal reform, women's suffrage, labor unions, and corporate controls.

There are, however, other reasons, not derived from any consideration merely of our rights, but arising out of the conditions of the South, and of the country—considerations which have already been referred to by Mr. Phillips—considerations which must arrest the attention of statesmen. I believe that when the tall heads of this Rebellion shall have been swept down, as they will be swept down, when the Davises and Toombses and Stephenses, and others who are leading this Rebellion shall have been blotted out, there will be this rank undergrowth of treason, to which reference has been made, growing up there, and interfering with, and thwarting the quiet operation of the Federal Government in those states. You will see those traitors, handing down, from sire to son, the same malignant spirit which they have manifested and which they are now exhibiting, with malicious hearts, broad blades, and bloody hands in the field, against our sons and brothers. That spirit will still remain; and whoever sees the Federal Government extended over those Southern States will see that Government in a strange land, and not only in a strange land, but in an enemy's land. A post-master of the United States in the South will find himself surrounded by a hostile spirit; a collector in a Southern port will find himself surrounded by a hostile spirit; a United States marshal or United States judge will be surrounded there by a hostile element. That enmity will not die out in a year, will not die out

A regiment of Free black Union soldiers, 1862.

in an age. The Federal Government will be looked upon in those States precisely as the Governments of Austria and France are looked upon in Italy at the present moment. They will endeavor to circumvent, they will endeavor to destroy, the peaceful operation of this Government. Now, where will you find the strength to counterbalance this spirit, if you do not find it in the Negroes of the South? They are your friends, and have always been your friends. They were your friends even when the Government did not regard them as such. They comprehended the genius of this war before you did. It is a significant fact, it is a marvellous fact, it seems almost to imply a direct interposition of Providence, that this war, which began in the interest of slavery on both sides, bids fair to end in the interest of liberty on both sides. [Applause.] It was begun, I say, in the interest of slavery on both sides. The South was fighting to take slavery out of the Union, and the North was fighting to keep it in the Union; the South fighting to get it beyond the limits of the United States Constitution, and the North fighting to retain it within those limits; the South fighting for new guarantees, and the North fighting for the old guarantees;—both despising the Negro, both insulting the Negro. Yet, the Negro, apparently endowed with wisdom from on high, saw more clearly the end from the beginning than we did. When Seward said the status of no man in the country would be changed by the war, the Negro did not believe him. [Applause.] When our generals sent their underlings in shoulder-straps to hunt the flying Negro back from our lines into the jaws of slavery, from which he had escaped, the Negroes thought that a mistake had been made, and that the intentions of the Government had not been rightly understood by our officers in shoulder-straps, and they continued to come into our lines, threading their way through bogs and fens, over briers and thorns, fording streams, swimming rivers, bringing us tidings as to the safe path to march, and pointing out the dangers that threatened us. They are our only friends in the South, and we should be true to them in this their trial hour, and see to it that they have the elective franchise.

I know that we are inferior to you in some things—virtually inferior. We walk about you like dwarfs among giants. Our heads are scarcely seen above the great sea of humanity. The Germans are superior to us; the Irish are superior to us; the Yankees are superior to us [Laughter]; they can do what we cannot, that is, what we have not hitherto been allowed to do. But while I make this admission, I utterly deny, that we are originally, or naturally, or practically, or in any way, or in any important sense, inferior to anybody on this globe. [Loud applause.] This charge of inferiority is an old dodge. It has been made available for oppression on many occasions. It is only about six centuries since the blue-eyed and fair-haired Anglo-Saxons were considered inferior by the haughty Normans, who once trampled upon them. If you read the history of the Norman Conquest, you will find that this proud Anglo-Saxon was once looked upon as of coarser clay than his Norman master, and might be found in the highways and byways of Old England laboring with a brass collar on his neck, and the name of his master marked upon it. You were down then! [Laughter and applause.] You are up now. I am glad you are up, and I want you to be glad to help us up also. [Applause.]

The story of our inferiority is an old dodge, as I have said; for wherever men oppress their fellows, wherever they enslave them, they will endeavor to find the needed apology for such enslavement and oppression in the character of the people oppressed and enslaved. When we wanted, a few years ago, a slice of Mexico, it was hinted that the Mexicans were an inferior race, that the old Castilian blood had become so weak that it would scarcely run down hill, and that Mexico needed the long, strong and beneficent arm of the Anglo-Saxon care extended over it. We said that it was necessary to its salvation, and a part of the "manifest destiny" of this Republic, to extend our arm over that dilapidated government. So, too, when Russia wanted to take possession of a part of the Ottoman Empire, the Turks were an "inferior race." So, too, when England wants to set the heel of her power more firmly in the quivering heart of old Ireland, the Celts are an "inferior race." So, too, the Negro, when he is to be robbed of any right which is justly his, is an "inferior man." It is said that we are ignorant; I admit it. But if we know enough to be hung, we know enough to vote. If the Negro knows enough to pay taxes to support the government, he knows enough to vote; taxation and representation should go together. If he knows enough to shoulder a musket and fight for the flag, fight for the government, he knows enough to vote. If he knows as much when he is sober as an Irishman knows when drunk, he knows enough to vote, on good American principles. [Laughter and applause.]

But I was saying that you needed a counterpoise in the persons of the slaves to the enmity that would exist at the South after the Rebellion is put down. I hold that the American people are bound, not only in self-defence, to extend this right to the freedmen of the South, but they are bound by their love of country, and by all their regard for the future safety of those Southern States, to do this—to do it as a measure essential to the preservation of peace there. But I will not dwell upon this. I put it to the American sense of honor. The honor of a nation is an important thing. It is said in the Scriptures, "What doth it profit a man if he gain the whole world, and lose his own soul?" It may be said, also, What doth it profit a nation if it gain the whole world, but lose its honor? I hold that the American government has taken upon itself a solemn obligation of honor, to see that this war—let it be long or short, let it cost much or let it cost little— that this war shall not cease until every freedman at the South has the right to vote. [Applause.] It has bound itself to it. What have you asked the black men of the South, the black men of the whole country to do? Why, you have asked them to incur the enmity of their masters, in order to befriend you and to befriend this Government. You have asked us to call down, not only upon ourselves, but upon our children's children, the deadly hate of the entire Southern people. You have called upon us to turn our backs upon our masters, to abandon their cause and espouse yours; to turn against the South and in favor of the North; to shoot down the Confederacy and uphold the flag—the American flag. You have called upon us to expose ourselves to all the subtle machinations of their malignity for all time. And now, what do you propose to do when you come to make peace? To reward your enemies, and trample in the dust your friends? Do you intend to sacrifice the very men who have come to the rescue of your banner in the South, and incurred the lasting displeasure of their masters thereby? Do you intend to sacrifice them and reward your enemies? Do you mean to give your enemies the right to vote, and take it away from your friends? Is that wise policy? Is that honorable? Could American honor withstand such a blow? I do not believe you will do it. I think you will see to it that we have the right to vote. There is something too mean in looking upon the Negro, when you are in trouble, as a citizen, and when you are free from trouble, as an alien. When this nation was in trouble, in its early struggles, it looked upon the Negro as a citizen. In 1776 he was a citizen. At the time of the formation of the Constitution the Negro had the right to vote in eleven States out of the old thirteen. In your trouble you have made us citizens. In 1812 Gen. Jackson addressed us as citizens—"fellow-citizens." He wanted us to fight. We were citizens then! And now, when you come to frame a conscription bill, the Negro is a citizen again. He has been a citizen just three times in the history of this government, and it has always been in time of trouble. In time of trouble we are citizens. Shall we be citizens in war, and aliens in peace? Would that be just?

I ask my friends who are apologizing for not insisting upon this right, where can the black man look, in this country, for the assertion of his right, if he may not look to the Massachusetts Anti-Slavery Society? Where under the whole heavens can he look for sympathy, in asserting this right, if he may not look to this platform? Have you lifted us up to a certain height to see that we are men, and then are any disposed to leave us there, without seeing that we are put in possession of all our rights? We look naturally to this platform for the assertion of all our rights, and for this one especially. I understand the anti-slavery societies of this country to be based on two principles—first, the freedom of the blacks of this country; and, second, the elevation of them. Let me not be misunderstood here. I am not asking for sympathy at the hands of abolitionists, sympathy at the hands of any. I think the American people are disposed often to be generous rather than just. I look over this country at the present time, and I see Educational Societies, Sanitary Commissions, Freedmen's Associations, and the like—all very good: but in regard to the colored people there is always more that is benevolent, I perceive, than just, manifested towards us. What I ask for the Negro is not benevolence, not pity, not sympathy, but simply justice. [Applause.]

A drawing of families greeting black Union soldiers returning after the war, circa 1865.

The American people have always been anxious to know what they shall do with us. Gen. Banks was distressed with solicitude as to what he should do with the Negro. Everybody has asked the question, and they learned to ask it early of the abolitionists, "What shall we do with the Negro?" I have had but one answer from the beginning. Do nothing with us! Your doing with us has already played the mischief with us. Do nothing with us! If the apples will not remain on the tree of their own strength, if they are wormeaten at the core, if they are early ripe and disposed to fall, let them fall! I am not for tying or fastening them on the tree in any way, except by nature's plan, and if they will not stay there, let them fall. And if the Negro cannot stand on his own legs, let him fall also. All I ask is, give him a chance to stand on his own legs! Let him alone! If you see him on his way to school, let him alone, don't disturb him! If you see him going to the dinner table at a hotel, let him go! If you see him going to the ballot box, let him alone, don't disturb him! [Applause.] If you see him going into a work-shop, just let him alone—your interference is doing him a positive injury. Gen. Banks' "preparation" is of a piece with this attempt to prop up the Negro. Let him fall if he cannot stand alone! If the Negro cannot live by the line of eternal justice, so beautifully pictured to you in the illustration used by Mr. Phillips, the fault will not be yours, it will be his who made the Negro, and established that line for his government. [Applause.] Let him live or die by that. If you will only untie his hands, and give him a chance, I think he will live. He will work as readily for himself as the white man. A great many delusions have been swept away by this war. One was, that the Negro would not work; he has proved his ability to work. Another was, that the Negro would not fight; that he possessed only the most sheepish attributes of humanity; was a perfect lamb, or an "Uncle Tom;" disposed to take off his coat whenever required, fold his hands, and be whipped by anybody who wanted to whip him. But the war has proved that there is a great deal of human nature in the Negro, and that "he will fight," as Mr. Quincy, our President, said, in earlier days than these, "when there is reasonable probability of his whipping anybody." [Laughter and applause.]

ON WOMEN'S RIGHT TO VOTE

Susan B. Anthony, 1873

A speech given some weeks after her arrest for casting an illegal vote in the presidential election, November 1, 1872. She was tried and then fined $100 but refused to pay.

Friends and fellow citizens: I stand before you tonight under indictment for the alleged crime of having voted at the last presidential election, without having a lawful right to vote. It shall be my work this evening to prove to you that in thus voting, I not only committed no crime, but, instead, simply exercised my citizen's rights, guaranteed to me and all United States citizens by the National Constitution, beyond the power of any state to deny.

The preamble of the Federal Constitution says:

"We, the people of the United States, in order to form a more perfect union, establish justice, insure domestic tranquillity, provide for the common defense, promote the general welfare, and secure the blessings of liberty to ourselves and our posterity, do ordain and establish this Constitution for the United States of America."

It was we, the people; not we, the white male citizens; nor yet we, the male citizens; but we, the whole people, who formed the Union. And we formed it, not to give the blessings of liberty, but to secure them; not to the half of ourselves and the half of our posterity, but to the whole people - women as well as men. And it is a downright mockery to talk to women of their enjoyment of the blessings of liberty while they are denied the use of the only means of securing them provided by this democratic-republican government - the ballot.

For any state to make sex a qualification that must ever result in the disfranchisement of one entire half of the people, is to pass a bill of attainder, or, an ex post facto law, and is therefore a violation of the supreme law of the land. By it the blessings of liberty are forever withheld from women and their female posterity.

To them this government has no just powers derived from the consent of the governed. To them this government is not a democracy. It is not a republic. It is an odious aristocracy; a hateful oligarchy of sex; the most hateful aristocracy ever established on the face of the globe; an oligarchy of wealth, where the rich govern the poor. An oligarchy of learning, where the educated govern the ignorant, or even an oligarchy of race, where the Saxon rules the African, might be endured; but this oligarchy of sex, which makes father, brothers, husband, sons, the oligarchs over the mother and sisters, the wife and daughters, of every household - which ordains all men sovereigns, all women subjects, carries dissension, discord, and rebellion into every home of the nation.

Webster, Worcester, and Bouvier all define a citizen to be a person in the United States, entitled to vote and hold office.

A portrait photograph taken about 1880 of Susan Brownell Anthony (1820–1906), at left, with Elizabeth Cady Stanton (1815–1902). American social reformers and leaders in women's suffrage, they had organized the National Woman Suffrage Association in 1869.

The only question left to be settled now is: Are women persons? And I hardly believe any of our opponents will have the hardihood to say they are not. Being persons, then, women are citizens; and no state has a right to make any law, or to enforce any old law, that shall abridge their privileges or immunities. Hence, every discrimination against women in the constitutions and laws of the several states is today null and void, precisely as is every one against Negroes.

Following her death in 1906 after five decades of tireless work, the Democratic and Republican parties both endorsed women's right to vote. In August of 1920, the 19th Amendment to the U.S. Constitution was finally ratified, allowing women to vote.

"I Feel that My Country Has Gotten a Bad Name"

Sitting Bull, August 1883

A select committee from the United States Senate was appointed to make a study on the condition of the Native American tribes in the territories of Montana and Dakota, under a resolution adopted in the Senate in the spring of 1883. While they were at the Standing Rock Agency in August of 1883, Sitting Bull appeared before the committee. Before Sitting Bull got down to the business of telling the committee what he thought about conditions for his people, this interesting repartee was entered in the official minutes:

CHAIRMAN: Ask Sitting Bull if he has anything to say to the committee.

SITTING BULL: Of course I will speak to you if you desire me to do so. I suppose it is only such men as you desire to speak who must say something.

CHAIRMAN: We supposed the Indians would select men to speak for them, but any man who desires to speak, or any man the Indians may desire shall talk for them. We will be glad to hear if he has anything to say.

SITTING BULL: Do you know who I am, that you speak of me as you do?

CHAIRMAN: I know that you are Sitting Bull, and if you have anything to say we will be glad to hear you.

SITTING BULL: Do you recognize me; do you know who I am?

CHAIRMAN: I know you are Sitting Bull.

SITTING BULL: You say you know I am Sitting Bull, but do you know the position I hold?

CHAIRMAN: I do not know any difference between you and the other Indians at this agency.

SITTING BULL: I am here by the will of the Great Spirit, and by his will I am a chief. My heart is red and sweet, and I know it is sweet, because whatever passes near me puts out its tongue to me; and yet you men have come here to talk with us, and you do not know who I am. I want to tell you that if the Great Spirit has chosen any one to be the chief of this country it is myself.

Later, Sitting Bull addressed the committee in this manner:

I feel that my country has gotten a bad name. I came in with a glad heart to shake hands with you, my friends, for I feel that I have displeased you. And here I am to apologize to you for my bad conduct and to take back what I said.

I will take it back because I consider I have made your hearts bad. I heard that you were coming here from the Great Father's house some time before you came, and I have been sitting here like a prisoner waiting for some one to release me. I was looking for you everywhere, and I considered that when we talked with you it was the same as if we were talking with the Great Father. And I believe that what I pour out from the heart the Great Father will hear.

What I take back is what I said to cause the people to leave the council, and want to apologize for leaving myself. The people acted like children, and I am sorry for it. I was very sorry when I found out that your intentions were good and entirely different from what I supposed they were.

Now I will tell you my mind and I will tell everything straight. I know the Great Spirit is looking down upon me from above, and will hear what I say, therefore I will do my best to talk straight. And I am in hopes that some one will listen to my wishes and help me to carry them out.

I have always been a chief, and have been made chief of all the land. Thirty-two years ago I was present at the councils with the white man, and at the time of the Fort Rice council I was on the prairie listening to it. And since then a

A photograph taken in 1880 of Chief Tatanka Yotaka or Sitting Bull (c.1834–1890). He led the Sioux in their resistance against the settlers. At the end of his life he toured as part of Buffalo Bill's Wild West Show.

great many questions have been asked me about it, and I always said, wait. And then the Black Hills council was held, and they asked me to give up that land, and I said they must wait. I remember well all the promises that were made about that land because I have thought a great deal about them since that time.

Of course, I know that the Great Spirit provided me with animals for my food, but I did not stay out on the prairie because I did not wish to accept the offers of the Great Father, for I sent in a great many of my people and I told them that the Great Father was providing for them and keeping his agreements with them. And I was sending the Indians word all the time I was out that they must remember their agreements and fulfill them, and carry them out straight.

When the English authorities were looking for me I heard that the Great Father's people were looking for me, too. I was not lost. I knew where I was going all the time. Previous to that time, when a Catholic priest called "White Hair" (meaning Bishop Marty) came to see me, I told him all these things plainly. He told me the wishes of the Great Father, and I made promises which I meant to fulfill, and did fulfill. And when I went over into the British possessions he followed me, and I told him everything that was in my heart, and sent him back to tell the Great Father what I told him.

Buffalo on the range in Custer State Park.

And General Terry sent me word afterwards to come in, because he had big promises to make me. And I sent him word that I would not throw my country away; that I considered it all mine still, and I wanted him to wait just four years for me; that I had gone over there to attend to some business of my own, and my people were doing just as any other people would do. If a man loses anything and goes back and looks carefully for it he will find it, and that is what the Indians are doing now when they ask you to give them the things that were promised them in the past. And I do not consider that they should be treated like beasts, and that is the reason I have grown up with the feelings I have.

Whatever you wanted of me I have obeyed, and I have come when you called me. The Great Father sent me word that whatever he had against me in the past had been forgiven and thrown aside, and he would have nothing against me in the future, and I accepted his promises and came in. And he told me not to step aside from the white man's path, and I told him I would not, and I am doing my best to travel in that path.

I feel that my country has gotten a bad name, and I want it to have a good name. It used to have a good name, and I sit sometimes and wonder who it is that has given it a bad name. You are the only people now who can give it a good name, and I want you to take good care of my country and respect it.

When we sold the Black Hills we got a very small price for it, and not what we ought to have received. I used to think that the size of the payments would remain the same all the time, but they are growing smaller all the time.

I want you to tell the Great Father everything I have said, and that we want some benefits from the promises he has made to us. And I don't think I should be tormented with anything about giving up any part of my land until those promises are fulfilled. I would rather wait until that time, when I will be ready to transact any business he may desire.

I consider that my country takes in the Black Hills, and runs from the Powder River to the

Missouri, and that all of this land belongs to me. Our reservation is not as large as we want it to be, and I suppose the Great Father owes us money now for land he has taken from us in the past.

You white men advise us to follow your ways, and therefore I talk as I do. When you have a piece of land, and anything trespasses on it, you catch it and keep it until you get damages, and I am doing the same thing now. And I want you to tell this to the Great Father for me. I am looking into the future for the benefit of my children, and that is what I mean, when I say I want my country taken care of for me.

My children will grow up here, and I am looking ahead for their benefit, and for the benefit of my children's children, too; and even beyond that again. I sit here and look around me now, and I see my people starving, and I want the Great Father to make an increase in the amount of food that is allowed us now, so that they may be able to live. We want cattle to butcher—I want to kill 300 head of cattle at a time. That is the way you live, and we want to live the same way. This is what I want you to tell the Great Father when you go back home.

If we get the things we want our children will be raised like the white children. When the Great Father told me to live like his people I told him to send me six teams of mules, because that is the way white people make a living, and I wanted my children to have these things to help them to make a living. I also told him to send me two spans of horses with wagons, and everything else my children would need. I also asked for a horse and buggy for my children. I was advised to follow the ways of the white man, and that is why I asked for those things.

I never ask for anything that is not needed. I also asked for a cow and a bull for each family, so that they can raise cattle of their own. I asked for four yokes of oxen and wagons with them also, a yoke of oxen and a wagon for each of my children to haul wood with.

It is your own doing that I am here. You sent me here, and advised me to live as you do, and it is not right for me to live in poverty. I asked the Great Father for hogs, male and female, and for male and female sheep for my children to raise from. I did not leave out anything in the way of animals that the white men have; I asked for every one of them. I want you to tell the Great Father to send me some agricultural implements, so that I will not be obliged to work barehanded.

Whatever he sends to this agency our agent will take care of for us, and we will be satisfied because we know he will keep everything right. Whatever is sent here for us he will be pleased to take care of for us. I want to tell you that our rations have been reduced to almost nothing, and many of the people have starved to death.

Now I beg of you to have the amount of rations increased so that our children will not starve, but will live better than they do now. I want clothing, too, and I will ask for that, too. We want all kinds of clothing for our people. Look at the men around here and see how poorly dressed they are. We want some clothing this month, and when it gets cold we want more to protect us from the weather.

That is all I have to say.

THE STAR SPANGLED BANNER

1 O say can you see, by the dawn's ear - ly light,
2 O thus be it ev - er, when free - men shall stand

what so proud - ly we hailed at the twi - light's last gleam - ing,
be - tween their loved homes and the war's des - o - lat - tion!

whose broad stripes and bright stars, through the per - il - lous fight,
Blest with vic - tory and peace, may the heaven-re - scued land

o'er the ram - parts we watched, were so gal - lant - ly stream - ing?
praise the Power that hath made and pre - served us a na - tion!

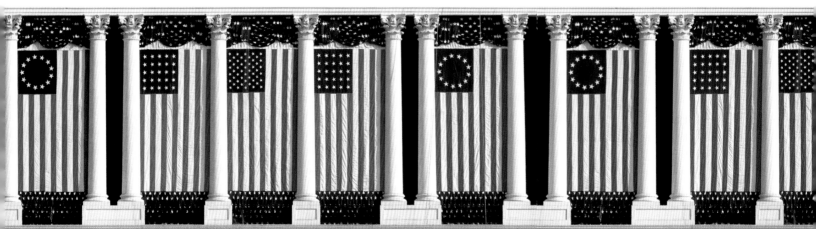

And the rock-ets' red glare, the bombs burst-ing in air,
Then ___ con-quer we must, when our cause it is just,

gave proof through the night that our flag was still there.
and this be our mot-to, "In God is our trust."

O ___ say does that star-span-gled ban-ner yet wave
And the star-span-gled ban-ner in tri-umph shall wave

o'er the land of the free and the home of the brave?
o'er the land of the free and the home of the brave!

Words: Francis Scott Key (1779-1843)
Music: *National Anthem*, source unknown, ca. 18th cent.

PART IV
CARRYING FREEDOM'S TORCH

The Statue of Liberty, created by French sculptor Frederic Auguste Bartholdi, arrived in New York Harbor in June 1885, in 350 pieces packed in 214 crates for the trip. It took four months to re-assemble.

America had difficulty raising money to build a pedestal until Joseph Pulitzer sounded off in the editorial page of his newspaper, The World. Pulitzer's barbs worked, the pedestal was financed by August 1885, and construction completed the following April. On October 28, 1886, the dedication of the Statue of Liberty took place in front of thousands of spectators—a centennial gift ten years late.

Emma Lazarus, the author of "The New Colossus," was born to a prominent Jewish family in New York City in 1849. At 25 she was a published author and poet. In 1883 she donated the poem for auction to help raise money for the Art Loan Fund Exhibition in Aid of the Bartholdi Pedestal Fund for the Statue of Liberty. In 1901 "The New Colossus" was inscribed on a bronze plaque and attached to the base of the statue.

Lady Liberty has become a beacon of hope, welcoming those from around the world to "the land of the free and the home of the brave." Thousands of those "masses longing to breathe free" have passed through the Ellis Island immigration offices.

THE NEW COLOSSUS

Sonnet for the Statue of Liberty, by Emma Lazarus

Not like the brazen giant of Greek fame,
With conquering limbs astride from land to land;
Here at our sea-washed, sunset gates shall stand
A mighty woman with a torch, whose flame
Is the imprisoned lightning, and her name
Mother of Exiles. From her beacon-hand
Glows world-wide welcome; her mild eyes command
The air-bridged harbor that twin cities frame.
"Keep ancient lands, your storied pomp!" cries she
With silent lips. "Give me your tired, your poor,
Your huddled masses yearning to breathe free,
The wretched refuse of your teeming shore.
Send these, the homeless, tempest-tost to me,
I lift my lamp beside the golden door!"

facing page: The interior of Ellis Island Museum.

You're A Grand Old Flag

George M. Cohan

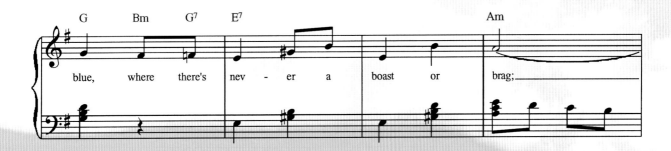

blue, where there's nev - er a boast or brag;

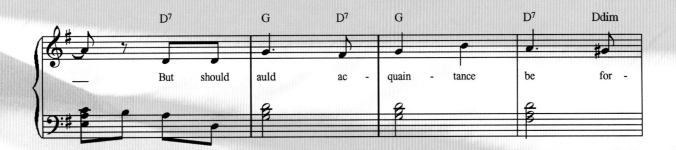

But should auld ac - quain - tance be for -

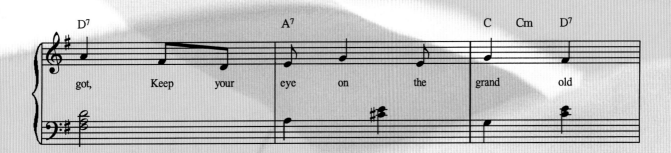

got, Keep your eye on the grand old

flag. You're a flag.

George M. Cohan (1878–1942) wrote many patriotic songs, but this is one of his earliest and best loved. He was just 16 when he sold his first song to Witmark Music Publishing. Over the course of his life he wrote more than 500 songs, many of which were major hits. The original title for this song was "You're a Grand Old Rag," but folks objected and Cohan renamed the tune.

WAR MESSAGE
TO CONGRESS

President Woodrow Wilson, April 2, 1917

We have no quarrel with the German people. We have no feeling towards them but one of sympathy and friendship. It was not upon their impulse that their government acted in entering this war. It was not with their previous knowledge or approval. It was a war determined upon as wars used to be determined upon in the old, unhappy days when peoples were nowhere consulted by their rulers and wars were provoked and waged in the interest of dynasties or of little groups of ambitious men who were accustomed to use their fellow men as pawns and tools. Self-governed nations do not fill their neighbour states with spies or set the course of intrigue to bring about some critical posture of affairs which will give them an opportunity to strike and make conquest. Such designs can be successfully worked out only under cover and where no one has the right to ask questions. Cunningly contrived plans of deception or aggression, carried, it may be, from generation to generation, can be worked out and kept from the light only within the privacy of courts or behind the carefully guarded confidences of a narrow and privileged class. They are happily impossible where public opinion commands and insists upon full information concerning all the nation's affairs.

A steadfast concert for peace can never be maintained except by a partnership of democratic nations. No autocratic government could be trusted to keep faith within it or observe its covenants. It must be a league of honour, a partnership of opinion. Intrigue would eat its vitals away; the plottings of inner circles who could plan what they would and render account to no one would be a corruption seated at its very heart. Only free peoples can hold their purpose and their honour steady to a common end and prefer the interests of mankind to any narrow interest of their own.

Just because we fight without rancor and without selfish object, seeking nothing for ourselves but what we shall wish to share with all free peoples, we shall, I feel confident, conduct our operations as belligerents without passion and ourselves observe with proud punctilio the principles of right and of fair play we profess to be fighting for.

We are now about to accept gauge of battle with this natural foe to liberty and shall, if necessary, spend the whole force of the nation to check and nullify its pretensions and its power. We are glad, now that we see the facts with no veil of false pretence about them, to fight thus for the ultimate peace of the world and for the liberation of its peoples, the German peoples included: for the rights of nations great and small and the privilege of men everywhere to choose their way of life and of obedience. The world must be made safe for democracy. Its peace must be planted upon the tested foundations of political liberty. We have no selfish ends to serve. We desire no conquest, no dominion. We seek no indemnities for ourselves, no material compensation for the sacrifices we shall freely make. We are but one of the champions of the rights of mankind. We shall be satisfied when those rights have been made as secure as the faith and the freedom of nations can make them.

1917—Uncle Sam points his accusing finger of moral responsibility in a recruitment poster for the American forces during World War I.

The pledge was written in August 1892, by Francis Bellamy, a Baptist minister. Bellamy meant the pledge to be: "an intensive communing with the salient points of our national history, from the Declaration of Independence onward." However, the pledge we recite today is a bit different from the one Bellamy composed. In 1923 the National Flag conference inserted "to the flag," and in 1954 Congress added the words "under God," making the Pledge a non-denominational prayer as well as a patriotic oath.

PLEDGE OF ALLEGIANCE

I Pledge Allegiance to the flag of the United States of America and to the Republic for which it stands, one Nation under God, indivisible, with liberty and justice for all.

THE AMERICAN'S CREED

"I believe in the United States of America as a Government of the people by the people, for the people, whose just powers are derived from the consent of the governed; a democracy in a Republic; a sovereign Nation of many sovereign States; a perfect Union, one and inseparable; established upon those principles of freedom, equality, justice, and humanity for which American patriots sacrificed their lives and fortunes.

I therefore believe it is my duty to my Country to love it; to support its Constitution; to obey its laws; to respect its flag, and to defend it against all enemies."

In 1917 William Tyler Page won a nationwide competition to compose a National Creed. The Creed was officially accepted by the House as the American's Creed on April 3, 1918. Tyler, an employee in the House, was elected Clerk of the U.S. House of Representatives, a position he held for the remainder of his life.

"THE FOUR FREEDOMS"

President Franklin Delano Roosevelt, January 6, 1941

In this excerpt from his State of the Union Address on January 6, 1941, President Roosevelt formulated a set of basic human rights which he called "The Four Freedoms". Roosevelt identified these freedoms as freedom of speech and expression, freedom of worship, freedom from want, and freedom from fear. As an agenda for foreign policy, they were in large part incorporated into the 1941 Atlantic Charter.

In the future days, which we seek to make secure, we look forward to a world founded upon four essential human freedoms.

The first is freedom of speech and expression—everywhere in the world.

The second is freedom of every person to worship God in his own way—everywhere in the world.

The third is freedom from want—which, translated into world terms, means economic understandings which will secure to every nation a healthy peacetime life for its inhabitants—everywhere in the world.

The fourth is freedom from fear—which, translated into world terms, means a world-wide reduction of armaments to such a point and in such a thorough fashion that no nation will be in a position to commit an act of physical aggression against any neighbor—anywhere in the world.

That is no vision of a distant millennium. It is a definite basis for a kind of world attainable in our own time and generation. That kind of world is the very antithesis of the so-called new order of tyranny which the dictators seek to create with the crash of a bomb.

To that new order we oppose the greater conception—the moral order. A good society is able to face schemes of world domination and foreign revolutions alike without fear.

Since the beginning of our American history, we have been engaged in change—in a perpetual peaceful revolution—a revolution which goes on steadily, quietly adjusting itself to changing conditions—without the concentration camp or the quick-lime in the ditch. The world order which we seek is the cooperation of free countries, working together in a friendly, civilized society.

This nation has placed its destiny in the hands and heads and hearts of its millions of free men and women; and its faith in freedom under the guidance of God. Freedom means the supremacy of human rights everywhere. Our support goes to those who struggle to gain those rights or keep them. Our strength is our unity of purpose.

To that high concept there can be no end save victory.

From *Congressional Record,* 1941, Vol. 87, Pt. I.

Franklin Delano Roosevelt, 32nd president of the United States.
His time in office was extended to three terms to maintain
consistent leadership throughout World War II.

"A Date Which Will Live in Infamy"

President Franklin Delano Roosevelt, December 8, 1941

Yesterday, December 7, 1941—a date which will live in infamy—the United States of America was suddenly and deliberately attacked by naval and air forces of the Empire of Japan.

The United States was at peace with that nation and, at the solicitation of Japan, was still in conversation with its Government and its Emperor looking toward the maintenance of peace in the Pacific. Indeed, one hour after Japanese air squadrons had commenced bombing in Oahu, the Japanese Ambassador to the United States and his colleague delivered to the Secretary of State a formal reply to a recent American message. While this reply stated that it seemed useless to continue the existing diplomatic negotiations, it contained no threat or hint of war or armed attack.

It will be recorded that the distance of Hawaii from Japan makes it obvious that the attack was deliberately planned many days or even weeks ago. During the intervening time the Japanese Government has deliberately sought to deceive the United States by false statements and expressions of hope for continued peace.

The attack yesterday on the Hawaiian Islands has caused severe damage to American naval and military forces. Very many American lives have been lost. In addition American ships have been reported torpedoed on the high seas between San Francisco and Honolulu.

Yesterday the Japanese Government also launched an attack against Malaya. Last night Japanese forces attacked Hong Kong. Last night Japanese forces attacked Guam. Last night Japanese forces attacked the Philippine Islands. Last night the Japanese attacked Wake Island. This morning the Japanese attacked Midway Island.

Japan has, therefore, undertaken a surprise offensive extending throughout the Pacific area. The facts of yesterday speak for themselves. The people of the United States have already formed their opinions and well understand the implications to the very life and safety of our nation.

As Commander-in-Chief of the Army and Navy, I have directed that all measures be taken for our defense.

Always will we remember the character of the onslaught against us. No matter how long it may take us to overcome this premeditated invasion, the American people in their righteous might will win through to absolute victory.

I believe I interpret the will of the Congress and of the people when I assert that we will not only defend ourselves to the uttermost but will make very certain that this form of treachery shall never endanger us again.

The Japanese attack on U.S. ships in Pearl Harbor, Hawaii, on December 7, 1941. The USS Maryland is next to the capsized USS Oklahoma, and the USS West Virginia is burning in the background. The Maryland was one of the first ships to rejoin the fleet after the bombardment.

Hostilities exist. There is no blinking at the fact that our people, our territory and our interests are in grave danger.

With confidence in our armed forces—with the unbounded determination of our people—we will gain the inevitable triumph—so help us God.

I ask that the Congress declare that since the unprovoked and dastardly attack by Japan on Sunday, December seventh, a state of war has existed between the United States and the Japanese Empire.

VICTORY ORDER OF THE DAY

General Dwight D. Eisenhower, May 8, 1945

As printed in The New York Times on Germany's defeat in the European theater of WW II.

The crusade on which we embarked in the early summer of 1944 has reached its glorious conclusion. It is my especial privilege, in the name of all nations represented in this theatre of war, to commend each of you for the valiant performance of duty.

Though these words are feeble, they come from the bottom of a heart overflowing with pride in your loyal service and admiration for you as warriors. Your accomplishments at sea, in the air, on the ground and in the field of supply have astonished the world.

Even before the final week of the conflict you had put 5,000,000 of the enemy permanently out of the war. You have taken in stride military tasks so difficult as to be classed by many doubters as impossible. You have confused, defeated and destroyed your savagely fighting foe. On the road to victory you have endured every discomfort and privation and have surmounted every obstacle that ingenuity and desperation could throw in your path. You did not pause until our front was firmly joined up with the great Red Army coming from the east and other Allied forces coming from the south.

Full victory in Europe has been attained. Working and fighting together in single and indestructible partnership you have achieved a perfection in the unification of air, ground and naval power that will stand as a model in our time.

The route you have traveled through hundreds of miles is marked by the graves of former comrades. From them have been exacted the ultimate sacrifice. The blood of many nations— American, British, Canadian, French, Polish and others—has helped to gain the victory. Each of the fallen died as a member of a team to which you belong, bound together by a common love of liberty and a refusal to submit to enslavement. No monument of stone, no memorial of whatever magnitude could so well express our respect and veneration for their sacrifice as would the perpetuation of the spirit of comradeship in which they died.

As we celebrate victory in Europe let us remind ourselves that our common problems of the immediate and distant future can be best solved in the same conceptions of cooperation and devotion to the cause of human freedom as have made this Expeditionary Force such a mighty engine of righteous destruction. Let us have no part in the profitless quarrels in which other men will inevitably engage as to what country and what service won the European war.

Every man and every woman of every nation here represented has served according to his or her ability and efforts and each has contributed to the outcome. This we shall remember and

Returning American hero, General Dwight D. Eisenhower, the Supreme Commander of Allied Forces in Europe, acknowledging the crowd as he is driven through the streets of Washington, D.C. on June 21, 1945. "Ike" Eisenhower served as President of the United States from 1952 to 1960.

in doing so we shall be revering each honored grave and be sending comfort to the loved ones of comrades who could not live to see this day.

FLAG OF THE FREE

By Walter Taylor Field

Look at the flag as it floats on high,
Streaming aloft in the clear, blue sky,
Rippling, leaping, tugging away,
Gay as the sunshine, bright as the day,
Throbbing with life, where the world may see—
Flag of our country, flag of the free!
What do we see in the flag on high,
That we bare our heads as it passes by,
That we thrill with pride, and our hearts beat fast,
And we cheer and cheer as the flag goes past—
The flag that waves for you and me
Flag of our country, flag of the free?

We see in the flag a nation's might.
The pledge of a safeguard day and night,
Of a watchful eye and a powerful arm
That guard the nation's homes from harm,
Of a strong defense on land and sea–
Flag of our country, flag of the free!
We see in the flag a union grand,
A brotherhood of heart and hand,
A pledge of love and a stirring call
To live our lives for the good of all—
Helpful and just and true to thee,
Flag of our country, flag of the free!

Flutter, dear flag, o'er the lands and the seas!
Fling out your stars and your stripes to the breeze,
Righting all wrongs, dispelling all fear,
Guarding the land that we cherish so dear,
And the God of our fathers, abiding with thee,
Will bless you and trust you, O flag of the free!

UNIVERSAL DECLARATION OF HUMAN RIGHTS

December 10, 1948

Whereas recognition of the inherent dignity and of the equal andinalienable rights of all members of the human family is the foundation of freedom, justice and peace in the world,

Whereas disregard and contempt for human rights have resulted in barbarous acts which have outraged the conscience of mankind, and the advent of a world in which human beings shall enjoy freedom of speech and belief and freedom from fear and want has been proclaimed as the highest aspiration of the common people,

Whereas it is essential, if man is not to be compelled to have recourse, as a last resort, to rebellion against tyranny and oppression, that human rights should be protected by the rule of law,

Whereas it is essential to promote the development of friendly relations between nations,

Whereas the peoples of the United Nations have in the Charter reaffirmed their faith in fundamental human rights, in the dignity and worth of the human person and in the equal rights of men and women and have determined to promote social progress and better standards of life in larger freedom,

Whereas Member States have pledged themselves to achieve, in cooperation with the United Nations, the promotion of universal respect for and observance of human rights and fundamental freedoms,

Whereas a common understanding of these rights and freedoms is of the greatest importance for the full realization of this pledge,

Now, therefore,

The General Assembly Proclaims this Universal Declaration of Human Rights as a common standard of achievement for all peoples and all nations, to the end that every individual and every organ of society, keeping this Declaration constantly in mind, shall strive by teaching and education to promote respect for these rights and freedoms and by progressive measures, national

Eleanor Roosevelt (1884–1962) at the United Nations in 1960. American author, lecturer, ambassador, social activist and wife of Franklin D. Roosevelt, the 32nd President, she regarded her work in helping to bring the Declaration of Human Rights to fruition as her greatest achievement.

and international, to secure their universal and effective recognition and observance, both among the peoples of Member States themselves and among the peoples of territories under their jurisdiction.

Article 1

All human beings are born free and equal in dignity and rights. They are endowed with reason and conscience and should act towards one another in a spirit of brotherhood.

Article 2

Everyone is entitled to all the rights and freedoms set forth in this Declaration, without distinction of any kind, such as race, color, sex, language, religion, political or other opinion, national or social origin, property, birth or other status.

Furthermore, no distinction shall be made on the basis of the political, jurisdictional or international status of the country or territory to which a person belongs, whether it be independent, trust, non-self-governing or under any other limitation of sovereignty.

Article 3

Everyone has the right to life, liberty and security of person.

Article 4

No one shall be held in slavery or servitude; slavery and the slave trade shall be prohibited in all their forms.

Article 5

No one shall be subjected to torture or to cruel, inhuman or degrading treatment or punishment.

Article 6

Everyone has the right to recognition everywhere as a person before the law.

Article 7

All are equal before the law and are entitled without any discrimination to equal protection of the law. All are entitled to equal protection against any discrimination in violation of the Declaration and against any incitement to such discrimination.

Article 8

Everyone has the right to an effective remedy by the competent national tribunals for acts violating the fundamental rights granted him by the constitution or by law.

Article 9

No one shall be subjected to arbitrary arrest, detention or exile.

Article 10

Everyone is entitled in full equality to a fair and public hearing by an independent and impartial tribunal, in the determination of his rights and obligations and of any criminal charge against him.

Article 11

1. Everyone charged with a penal offence has the right to be presumed innocent until proved guilty according to law in a public trial at which he has had all the guarantees necessary for his defence.

2. No one shall be held guilty of any penal offence on account of any act or omission which did not constitute a penal offence, under national or international law, at the time it was committed. Nor shall a heavier penalty be imposed than the one that was applicable at the time the penal offence was committed.

Article 12
No one shall be subjected to arbitrary interference with his privacy, family, home or correspondence, nor to attacks upon his honour and reputation. Everyone has the right to the protection of the law against such interference or attacks.

Article 13
1. Everyone has the right to freedom of movement and residence within the borders of each state.

2. Everyone has the right to leave any country, including his own, and to return to his country.

Article 14
1. Everyone has the right to seek and to enjoy in other countries asylum from persecution.

2. This right may not be invoked in the case of prosecutions genuinely arising from non-political crimes or from acts contrary to the purposes and principles of the United Nations.

Article 15
1. Everyone has the right to a nationality.

2. No one shall be arbitrarily deprived of his nationality nor denied the right to change his nationality.

Article 16
1. Men and women of full age, without any limitation due to race, nationality or religion, have the right to marry and to found a family. They are entitled to equal rights as to marriage, during marriage and at its dissolution.

2. Marriage shall be entered into only with the free and full consent of the intending spouses.

3. The family is the natural and fundamental group unit of society and is entitled to protection by society and the State.

Article 17
1. Everyone has the right to own property alone as well as in association with others.

2. No one shall be arbitrarily deprived of his property.

Article 18
Everyone has the right to freedom of thought, conscience and religion; this right includes freedom to change his religion or belief, and freedom, either alone or in community with others and in public or private, to manifest his religion or belief in teaching, practice, worship and observance.

Article 19

Everyone has the right to freedom of opinion and expression: this right includes freedom to hold opinions without interference and to seek, receive and impart information and ideas through any media and regardless of frontiers.

Article 20

1. Everyone has the right to freedom of peaceful assembly and association.

2. No one may be compelled to belong to an association.

Article 21

1. Everyone has the right to take part in the government of his country, directly or through freely chosen representatives.

2. Everyone has the right of equal access to public service in his country.

3. The will of the people shall be the basis of the authority of government; this will shall be expressed in periodic and genuine elections which shall be by universal and equal suffrage and shall be held by secret vote or by equivalent free voting procedures.

Article 22

Everyone, as a member of society, has the right to social security and is entitled to realization, through national effort and international co-operation and in accordance with the organization and resources of each State, of the economic, social and cultural rights indispensable for his dignity and the free development of his personality.

Article 23

1. Everyone has the right to work, to free choice of employment, to just and favourable conditions of work and to protection against unemployment.

2. Everyone, without any discrimination, has the right to equal pay for equal work.

3. Everyone who works has the right to just and favourable remuneration ensuring for himself and his family an existence worthy of human dignity, and supplemented, if necessary, by other means of social protection.

4. Everyone has the right to form and to join trade unions for the protection of his interests.

Article 24

Everyone has the right to rest and leisure, including reasonable limitation of working hours and periodic holidays with pay.

Article 25

1. Everyone has the right to a standard of living adequate for the health and well-being of himself and of his family, including food, clothing, housing and medical care and necessary social services, and the right to security in the event of unemployment, sickness, disability, widowhood, old age or other lack of livelihood in circumstances beyond his control.

2. Motherhood and childhood are entitled to special care and assistance. All children, whether born in or out of wedlock, shall enjoy the same social protection.

Article 26

1. Everyone has the right to education. Education shall be free, at least in the elementary and fundamental stages. Elementary education shall be compulsory. Technical and professional education shall be made generally available and higher education shall be equally accessible to all on the basis of merit.

2. Education shall be directed to the full development of the human personality and to the strengthening of respect for human rights and fundamental freedoms. It shall promote understanding, tolerance and friendship among all nations, racial or religious groups, and shall further the activities of the United Nations for the maintenance of peace.

3. Parents have a prior right to choose the kind of education that shall be given to their children.

Article 27

1. Everyone has the right freely to participate in the cultural life of the community, to enjoy the arts and to share in scientific advancement and its benefits.

2. Everyone has the right to the protection of the moral and material interests resulting from any scientific, literary or artistic production of which he is the author.

Article 28

Everyone is entitled to a social and international order in which the rights and freedoms set forth in this Declaration can be fully realized.

Article 29

1. Everyone has duties to the community in which alone the free and full development of his personality is possible.

2. In the exercise of his rights and freedoms, everyone shall be subject only to such limitations as are determined by law solely for the purpose of securing due recognition and respect for the rights and freedoms of others and of meeting the just requirements of morality, public order and the general welfare in a democratic society.

3. These rights and freedoms may in no case be exercised contrary to the purposes and principles of the United Nations.

Article 30

Nothing in this Declaration may be interpreted as implying for any State, group or person any right to engage in any activity or to perform any act aimed at the destruction of any of the rights and freedoms set forth herein.

Adopted by UN General Assembly Resolution 217A (III)

AMERICA THE BEAUTIFUL

Anthem

Purple mountain majesty in the Teton Mountains.

1 O beau-ti-ful for spa-cious skies, for am-ber waves of grain,
2 O beau-ti-ful for he-roes proved in lib-er-at-ing strife,
3 O beau-ti-ful for pa-triot dream that sees be-yond the years

for pur-ple moun-tain ma-jes-ties a-bove the fruit-ed plain!
who more than self their coun-try loved, and mer-cy more than life!
thine al-a-bas-ter ci-ties gleam, un-dimmed by hu-man tears!

A-mer-i-ca! A-mer-i-ca! God shed his grace on thee,
A-mer-i-ca! A-mer-i-ca! God mend thine ev-ery flaw,
A-mer-i-ca! A-mer-i-ca! God shed his grace on thee,

and crown thy good with bro-ther-hood from sea to shin-ing sea.
con-firm thy soul in self-con-trol, thy lib-er-ty in law.
and crown thy good with bro-ther-hood from sea to shin-ing sea.

Words: Katherine Lee Bates (1859-1929), alt.
Music: *Materna*, Samuel Augustus Ward (1848-1903)

PART V
LET FREEDOM RING

"Ask Not What your Country Can Do for You"

John F. Kennedy's Inaugural Address, January 20, 1961

Vice President Johnson, Mr. Speaker, Mr. Chief Justice, President Eisenhower, Vice President Nixon, President Truman, reverend clergy, fellow citizens, we observe today not a victory of party, but a celebration of freedom—symbolizing an end, as well as a beginning—signifying renewal, as well as change. For I have sworn before you and Almighty God the same solemn oath our forebears prescribed nearly a century and three quarters ago.

The world is very different now. For man holds in his mortal hands the power to abolish all forms of human poverty and all forms of human life. And yet the same revolutionary beliefs for which our forebears fought are still at issue around the globe—the belief that the rights of man come not from the generosity of the state, but from the hand of God.

We dare not forget today that we are the heirs of that first revolution. Let the word go forth from this time and place, to friend and foe alike, that the torch has been passed to a new generation of Americans—born in this century, tempered by war, disciplined by a hard and bitter peace, proud of our ancient heritage—and unwilling to witness or permit the slow undoing of those human rights to which this Nation has always been committed, and to which we are committed today at home and around the world.

Let every nation know, whether it wishes us well or ill, that we shall pay any price, bear any burden, meet any hardship, support any friend, oppose any foe, in order to assure the survival and the success of liberty.

This much we pledge—and more.

To those old allies whose cultural and spiritual origins we share, we pledge the loyalty of faithful friends. United, there is little we cannot do in a host of cooperative ventures. Divided, there is little we can do—for we dare not meet a powerful challenge at odds and split asunder.

To those new States whom we welcome to the ranks of the free, we pledge our word that one form of colonial control shall not have passed away merely to be replaced by a far more iron tyranny. We shall not always expect to find them supporting our view. But we shall always hope to find them strongly supporting their own freedom—and to remember that, in the past, those who foolishly sought power by riding the back of the tiger ended up inside.

To those peoples in the huts and villages across the globe struggling to break the bonds of mass misery, we pledge our best efforts to help them help themselves, for whatever period is required—not because the Communists may be doing it, not because we seek their votes, but because it is right. If a free society cannot help the many who are poor, it cannot save the few who are rich.

To our sister republics south of our border, we offer a special pledge—to convert our good words into good deeds—in a new alliance for progress—to assist free men and free governments in casting off the chains of poverty. But this peaceful revolution of hope cannot become the prey of hostile powers. Let all our neighbors know that we shall join with them to oppose aggression or subversion anywhere in the Americas. And let every other power know that this Hemisphere intends to remain the master of its own house.

To that world assembly of sovereign states, the United Nations, our last best hope in an age where the instruments of war have far outpaced the instruments of peace, we renew our pledge of support—to prevent it from becoming merely a forum for invective—to strengthen its shield of the new and the weak—and to enlarge the area in which its writ may run.

Finally, to those nations who would make themselves our adversary, we offer not a pledge but a request: that both sides begin anew the quest for peace, before the dark powers of destruction unleashed by science engulf all humanity in planned or accidental self-destruction.

We dare not tempt them with weakness. For only when our arms are sufficient beyond doubt can we be certain beyond doubt that they will never be employed.

But neither can two great and powerful groups of nations take comfort from our present course—both sides overburdened by the cost of modern weapons, both rightly alarmed by the steady spread of the deadly atom, yet both racing to alter that uncertain balance of terror that stays the hand of mankind's final war.

A 1960 photograph of the 35th president of the United States, John Fitzgerald Kennedy (1917–1963). His presidential career spanned the Bay of Pigs invasion, the Cuban Missile Crisis, and the building of the Berlin Wall, but was cut short when he was assassinated in Dallas, Texas on November 22, 1963.

So let us begin anew—remembering on both sides that civility is not a sign of weakness, and sincerity is always subject to proof. Let us never negotiate out of fear. But let us never fear to negotiate.

Let both sides explore what problems unite us instead of belaboring those problems which divide us.

Let both sides, for the first time, formulate serious and precise proposals for the inspection and control of arms—and bring the absolute power to destroy other nations under the absolute control of all nations.

Let both sides seek to invoke the wonders of science instead of its terrors. Together let us explore the stars, conquer the deserts, eradicate disease, tap the ocean depths, and encourage the arts and commerce.

Let both sides unite to heed in all corners of the earth the command of Isaiah—to "undo the heavy burdens ... and to let the oppressed go free."

And if a beachhead of cooperation may push back the jungle of suspicion, let both sides join in creating a new endeavor, not a new balance of power, but a new world of law, where the strong are just and the weak secure and the peace preserved.

All this will not be finished in the first 100 days. Nor will it be finished in the first 1,000 days, nor in the life of this Administration, nor even perhaps in our lifetime on this planet. But let us begin.

In your hands, my fellow citizens, more than in mine, will rest the final success or failure of our course. Since this country was founded, each generation of Americans has been summoned to give testimony to its national loyalty. The graves of young Americans who answered the call to service surround the globe.

Now the trumpet summons us again—not as a call to bear arms, though arms we need; not as a call to battle, though embattled we are—but a call to bear the burden of a long twilight struggle, year in and year out, "rejoicing in hope, patient in tribulation"—a struggle against the common enemies of man: tyranny, poverty, disease, and war itself.

Can we forge against these enemies a grand and global alliance, North and South, East and West, that can assure a more fruitful life for all mankind? Will you join in that historic effort?

In the long history of the world, only a few generations have been granted the role of defending freedom in its hour of maximum danger. I do not shrink from this responsibility—I welcome it. I do not believe that any of us would exchange places with any other people or any other generation. The energy, the faith, the devotion which we bring to this endeavor will light our country and all who serve it—and the glow from that fire can truly light the world.

And so, my fellow Americans: ask not what your country can do for you—ask what you can do for your country.

My fellow citizens of the world: ask not what America will do for you, but what together we can do for the freedom of man.

Finally, whether you are citizens of America or citizens of the world, ask of us the same high standards of strength and sacrifice which we ask of you. With a good conscience our only sure reward, with history the final judge of our deeds, let us go forth to lead the land we love, asking His blessing and His help, but knowing that here on earth God's work must truly be our own.

"I Have a Dream"

Martin Luther King, Jr., August 28, 1963

Five score years ago, a great American, in whose symbolic shadow we stand, signed the Emancipation Proclamation. This momentous decree came as a great beacon light of hope to millions of Negro slaves who had been seared in the flames of withering injustice. It came as a joyous daybreak to end the long night of captivity.

But one hundred years later, we must face the tragic fact that the Negro is still languishing in the corners of American society and finds himself an exile in his own land. So we have come here today to dramatize an appalling condition.

American civil rights activist Dr. Martin Luther King, Jr. (1929–1968) delivering his famous
"I have a dream" speech in front of the Lincoln Memorial on August 28, 1963.

In a sense we have come to our nation's capital to cash a check. When the architects of our republic wrote the magnificent words of the Constitution and the Declaration of Independence, they were signing a promissory note to which every American was to fall heir. This note was a promise that all men would be guaranteed the unalienable rights of life, liberty, and the pursuit of happiness.

It is obvious today that America has defaulted on this promissory note insofar as her citizens of color are concerned. Instead of honoring this sacred obligation, America has given the Negro people a bad check—a check which has come back marked "insufficient funds." But we refuse to believe that the bank of justice is bankrupt. We refuse to believe that there are insufficient funds in the great vaults of opportunity of this nation. So we have come to cash this check—a check that will give us upon demand the riches of freedom and the security of justice. We have also come to this hallowed spot to remind America of the fierce urgency of now. This is no time to engage in the luxury of cooling off or to take the tranquilizing drug of gradualism. Now is the time to make real the promises of democracy. Now is the time to rise from the dark and desolate valley of segregation to the sunlit path of racial justice. Now is the time to open the doors of opportunity to all of God's children. Now is the time to lift our nation from the quicksands of racial injustice to the solid rock of brotherhood.

It would be fatal for the nation to overlook the urgency of the moment and to underestimate the determination of the Negro. This sweltering summer of the Negro's legitimate discontent will not pass until there is an invigorating autumn of freedom and equality. Nineteen sixty-three is not an end, but a beginning. Those who hope that the Negro needed to blow off steam and will now be content will have a rude awakening if the nation returns to business as usual. There will be neither rest nor tranquility in America until the Negro is granted his citizenship rights. The whirlwinds of revolt will continue to shake the foundation of our nation until the bright day of justice emerges.

But there is something that I must say to my people who stand on the warm threshold which leads into the palace of justice. In the process of gaining our rightful place we must not be guilty of wrongful deeds. Let us not seek to satisfy our thirst for freedom by drinking from the cup of bitterness and hatred.

We must forever conduct our struggle on the high plane of dignity and discipline. Again and again we must rise to the majestic heights of meeting physical force with soul force. The marvelous new militancy which has engulfed the Negro community must not lead us to a distrust of all white people, for many of our white brothers, as evidenced by their presence here today, have come to realize that their destiny is tied up with our destiny and their freedom is inextricably bound to our freedom. We can not walk alone.

And as we walk, we must make the pledge that we shall march ahead. We cannot turn back. There are those who are asking the devotees of civil rights, "when will you be satisfied?" We can never be satisfied as long as the Negro is the victim of unspeakable horrors of police brutality. We can never be satisfied as long as our bodies, heavy with the fatigue of travel, cannot gain lodging in the motels of the highways and the hotels of the cities. We cannot be satisfied as long as the Negro's basic mobility is from a smaller ghetto to a larger one. We can never be satisfied as long as a Negro in Mississippi cannot vote and a Negro in New York believes he has nothing for which to vote. No, no, we are not satisfied, and we will not be satisfied until justice rolls down like waters and righteousness like a mighty stream.

I am not unmindful that some of you have come here out of great trials and tribulations. Some of you have come fresh from narrow cells. Some of you have come from areas where your quest for freedom left you battered by the storms of persecution and staggered by the winds of police brutality. You have been the veterans of creative suffering. Continue to work with the faith that unearned suffering is redemptive.

Go back to Mississippi, go back to Alabama, go back to South Carolina, go back to Georgia, go back to Louisiana, go back to the slums and ghettos of our northern cities, knowing that somehow this situation can and will be changed. Let us not wallow in the valley of despair.

I say to you today, my friends, that in spite of the difficulties and frustrations of the moment I still have a dream. It is a dream deeply rooted in the American dream.

I have a dream that one day this nation will rise up and live out the true meaning of its creed—"We hold these truths to be self evident, that all men are created equal."

I have a dream that one day on the red hills of Georgia the sons of former slaves and the sons of former slaveowners will be able to sit down together at the table of brotherhood.

I have a dream that one day even the state of Mississippi, a desert state sweltering with the heat of injustice and oppression, will be transformed into an oasis of freedom and justice.

I have a dream that my four little children will one day live in a nation where they will not be judged by the color of their skin but by the content of their character.

I have a dream today.

The King center erected in honor and in memory of Martin Luther King, Jr., who was assassinated by James Ruby in Memphis, Tennessee on April 4, 1968.

I have a dream that one day the state of Alabama, whose governor's lips are presently dripping with the words of interposition and nullification, will be transformed into a situation where little black boys and black girls will be able to join hands with little white boys and white girls and walk together as sisters and brothers.

I have a dream today.

I have a dream that one day every valley shall be exalted, every hill and mountain shall be made low, and rough places will be made plains, and the crooked places will be made straight, and the glory of the Lord shall be revealed, and all flesh shall see it together.

This is our hope. This is the faith with which I return to the south. With this faith we will be able to hew out of the mountain of despair a stone of hope. With this faith we will be able to transform the jangling discords of our nation into a beautiful symphony of brotherhood. With this faith we will be able to work together, to pray together, to struggle together, to go to jail together, to stand up for freedom together, knowing that we will be free one day.

This will be the day when all of God's children will be able to sing with a new meaning "My country 'tis of thee, sweet land of liberty, of thee I sing. Land where my fathers died, land of the pilgrim's pride, from every mountainside, let freedom ring."

And if America is to be a great nation this must come true. So let freedom ring from the prodigious hilltops of New Hampshire. Let freedom ring from the mighty mountains of New York. Let freedom ring from the heightening Alleghenies of Pennsylvania.

Let freedom ring from the snowcapped Rockies of Colorado.

Let freedom ring from the curvaceous peaks of California.

But not only that—let freedom ring from Stone Mountain in Georgia.

Let freedom ring from Lookout Mountain of Tennessee.

Let freedom ring from every hill and molehill of Mississippi. From every mountainside, let freedom ring.

When we let freedom ring, when we let it ring from every village and every hamlet, from every state and every city, we will be able to speed up that day when all of God's children, black men and white men, Jews and gentiles, Protestants and Catholics, will be able to join hands and sing in the words of the old Negro spiritual,

"Free at last! Free at last! Thank God Almighty, we are free at last!"

"THE GREAT SOCIETY"

President Lyndon B. Johnson, May 22, 1964

Commencement address given at the University of Michigan.

President Hatcher, Governor Romney, Senators McNamara and Hart, Congressmen Meader and Staebler, and other members of the fine Michigan delegation, members of the graduating class, my fellow Americans:

It is a great pleasure to be here today. This university has been coeducational since 1870, but I do not believe it was on the basis of your accomplishments that a Detroit high school girl said, "In choosing a college, you first have to decide whether you want a coeducational school or an educational school."

Well, we can find both here at Michigan, although perhaps at different hours.

I came out here today very anxious to meet the Michigan student whose father told a friend of mine that his son's education had been a real value. It stopped his mother from bragging about him.

I have come today from the turmoil of your Capital to the tranquility of your campus to speak about the future of your country.

The purpose of protecting the life of our Nation and preserving the liberty of our citizens is to pursue the happiness of our people. Our success in that pursuit is the test of our success as a Nation.

For a century we labored to settle and to subdue a continent. For half a century we called upon unbounded invention and untiring industry to create an order of plenty for all of our people.

The challenge of the next half century is whether we have the wisdom to use that wealth to

Detroit, Michigan.

enrich and elevate our national life, and to advance the quality of our American civilization.

Your imagination, your initiative, and your indignation will determine whether we build a society where progress is the servant of our needs, or a society where old values and new visions are buried under unbridled growth. For in your time we have the opportunity to move not only toward the rich society and the powerful society, but upward to the Great Society.

The Great Society rests on abundance and liberty for all. It demands an end to poverty and racial injustice, to which we are totally committed in our time. But that is just the beginning.

The Great Society is a place where every child can find knowledge to enrich his mind and to enlarge his talents. It is a place where leisure is a welcome chance to build and reflect, not a feared cause of boredom and restlessness. It is a place where the city of man serves not only the needs of the body and the demands of commerce but the desire for beauty and the hunger for community.

It is a place where man can renew contact with nature. It is a place which honors creation for its own sake and for what it adds to the understanding of the race. It is a place where men are more concerned with the quality of their goals than the quantity of their goods.

But most of all, the Great Society is not a safe harbor, a resting place, a final objective, a finished work. It is a challenge constantly renewed, beckoning us toward a destiny where the meaning of our lives matches the marvelous products of our labor.

So I want to talk to you today about three places where we begin to build the Great Society — in our cities, in our countryside, and in our classrooms.

Many of you will live to see the day, perhaps 50 years from now, when there will be 400 million Americans — four-fifths of them in urban areas. In the remainder of this century urban population will double, city land will double, and we will have to build homes, highways, and facilities equal to all those built since this country was first settled. So in the next 40 years we must re-build the entire urban United States.

Aristotle said: "Men come together in cities in order to live, but they remain together in order to live the good life." It is harder and harder to live the good life in American cities today.

The catalog of ills is long: there is the decay of the centers and the despoiling of the suburbs. There is not enough housing for our people or transportation for our traffic. Open land is vanishing and old landmarks are violated.

Worst of all expansion is eroding the precious and time honored values of community with neighbors and communion with nature. The loss of these values breeds loneliness and boredom and indifference.

Our society will never be great until our cities are great. Today the frontier of imagination and innovation is inside those cities and not beyond their borders.

A view of Lake Michigan.

New experiments are already going on. It will be the task of your generation to make the American city a place where future generations will come, not only to live but to live the good life.

I understand that if I stayed here tonight I would see that Michigan students are really doing their best to live the good life.

This is the place where the Peace Corps was started. It is inspiring to see how all of you, while you are in this country, are trying so hard to live at the level of the people.

A second place where we begin to build the Great Society is in our countryside. We have always prided ourselves on being not only America the strong and America the free, but America the beautiful. Today that beauty is in danger. The water we drink, the food we eat, the very air that we breathe, are threatened with pollution. Our parks are overcrowded, our seashores overburdened. Green fields and dense forests are disappearing.

A few years ago we were greatly concerned about the "Ugly American." Today we must act to prevent an ugly America.

For once the battle is lost, once our natural splendor is destroyed, it can never be recaptured. And once man can no longer walk with beauty or wonder at nature his spirit will wither and his sustenance be wasted.

A third place to build the Great Society is in the classrooms of America. There your children's lives will be shaped. Our society will not be great until every young mind is set free to scan the farthest reaches of thought and imagination. We are still far from that goal.

Today, 8 million adult Americans, more than the entire population of Michigan, have not finished 5 years of school. Nearly 20 million have not finished 8 years of school. Nearly 54 million — more than one quarter of all America — have not even finished high school.

Each year more than 100,000 high school graduates, with proved ability, do not enter college because they cannot afford it. And if we cannot educate today's youth, what will we do in 1970 when elementary school enrollment will be 5 million greater than 1960? And high school enrollment will rise by 5 million. College enrollment will increase by more than 3 million.

In many places, classrooms are overcrowded and curricula are outdated. Most of our qualified teachers are underpaid, and many of our paid teachers are unqualified. So we must give every child a place to sit and a teacher to learn from. Poverty must not be a bar to learning, and learning must offer an escape from poverty.

But more classrooms and more teachers are not enough. We must seek an educational system which grows in excellence as it grows in size. This means better training for our teachers. It means preparing youth to enjoy their hours of leisure as well as their hours of labor. It means exploring new techniques of teaching, to find new ways to stimulate the love of learning and the capacity for creation.

These are three of the central issues of the Great Society. While our Government has many programs directed at those issues, I do not pretend that we have the full answer to those problems.

The Johnson Space Center, Houston, Texas.

But I do promise this: We are going to assemble the best thought and the broadest knowledge from all over the world to find those answers for America. I intend to establish working groups to prepare a series of White House conferences and meetings — on the cities, on natural beauty, on the quality of education, and on other emerging challenges. And from these meetings and from this inspiration and from these studies we will begin to set our course toward the Great Society.

The solution to these problems does not rest on a massive program in Washington, nor can it rely solely on the strained resources of local authority. They require us to create new concepts of cooperation, a creative federalism, between the National Capital and the leaders of local communities.

Woodrow Wilson once wrote: "Every man sent out from his university should be a man of his Nation as well as a man of his time."

Within your lifetime powerful forces, already loosed, will take us toward a way of life beyond the realm of our experience, almost beyond the bounds of our imagination.

For better or for worse, your generation has been appointed by history to deal with those problems and to lead America toward a new age. You have the chance never before afforded to any people in any age. You can help build a society where the demands of morality, and the needs of the spirit, can be realized in the life of the Nation.

So, will you join in the battle to give every citizen the full equality which God enjoins and the law requires, whatever his belief, or race, or the color of his skin?

Will you join in the battle to give every citizen an escape from the crushing weight of poverty?

Will you join in the battle to make it possible for all nations to live in enduring peace — as neighbors and not as mortal enemies?

Will you join in the battle to build the Great Society, to prove that our material progress is only the foundation on which we will build a richer life of mind and spirit?

There are those timid souls who say this battle cannot be won; that we are condemned to a soulless wealth. I do not agree. We have the power to shape the civilization that we want. But we need your will, your labor, your hearts, if we are to build that kind of society.

Those who came to this land sought to build more than just a new country. They sought a new world. So I have come here today to your campus to say that you can make their vision our reality. So let us from this moment begin our work so that in the future men will look back and say: It was then, after a long and weary way, that man turned the exploits of his genius to the full enrichment of his life.

Thank you. Good-bye.

A license for the Great Society.

"WE SHALL OVERCOME"

President Lyndon B. Johnson, March 15, 1965

In this very eloquent speech to the full Congress, President Lyndon B. Johnson used the phrase "we shall overcome," borrowed from African-American leaders struggling for equal rights.

The speech was made a week after deadly racial violence erupted in Selma, Alabama, as African-Americans were attacked by police while preparing to march to Montgomery to protest voting rights discrimination.

The 36th president of the United States, Lyndon Baines Johnson (1908–1973) in 1965. He was sworn in only hours after the assassination of John F. Kennedy in 1963, on the presidential jet, Air Force One.

Discrimination took the form of literacy, knowledge or character tests administered solely to African-Americans to keep them from registering to vote.

Civil rights leader Rev. Martin Luther King and over 500 supporters planned to march from Selma to Montgomery to register African-Americans to vote. The police violence that erupted resulted in the death of a King supporter, a white Unitarian Minister from Boston named James J. Reeb.

A second attempt to march to Montgomery was also blocked by police. It took Federal intervention with the 'federalizing' of the Alabama National Guard and the addition of over 2000 other guards to ensure protection and allow the march to begin.

On March 21, 1965, the march to Montgomery finally began with over 3000 participants, under the glare of worldwide news publicity.

I speak tonight for the dignity of man and the destiny of Democracy. I urge every member of both parties, Americans of all religions and of all colors, from every section of this country, to join me in that cause.

At times, history and fate meet at a single time in a single place to shape a turning point in man's unending search for freedom. So it was at Lexington and Concord. So it was a century ago at Appomattox. So it was last week in Selma, Alabama. There, long suffering men and women peacefully protested the denial of their rights as Americans. Many of them were brutally assaulted. One good man—a man of God—was killed.

There is no cause for pride in what has happened in Selma. There is no cause for self-satisfaction in the long denial of equal rights of millions of Americans. But there is cause for hope and for faith in our Democracy in what is happening here tonight. For the cries of pain and the hymns and protests of oppressed people have summoned into convocation all the majesty of this great government—the government of the greatest nation on earth. Our mission is at once the oldest and the most basic of this country—to right wrong, to do justice, to serve man. In our time we have come to live with the moments of great crises. Our lives have been marked with debate about great issues, issues of war and peace, issues of prosperity and depression.

But rarely in any time does an issue lay bare the secret heart of America itself. Rarely are we met with a challenge, not to our growth or abundance, or our welfare or our security, but rather to the values and the purposes and the meaning of our beloved nation. The issue of equal rights for American Negroes is such an issue. And should we defeat every enemy, and should we double our wealth and conquer the stars, and still be unequal to this issue, then we will have failed as a people and as a nation. For, with a country as with a person, "what is a man profited if he shall gain the whole world, and lose his own soul?"

There is no Negro problem. There is no Southern problem. There is no Northern problem. There is only an American problem.

And we are met here tonight as Americans—not as Democrats or Republicans; we're met here as Americans to solve that problem. This was the first nation in the history of the world to be founded with a purpose.

The great phrases of that purpose still sound in every American heart, North and South: "All men are created equal." "Government by consent of the governed." "Give me liberty or give me death." And those are not just clever words, and those are not just empty theories. In their name Americans have fought and died for two centuries and tonight around the world they stand there as guardians of our liberty risking their lives. Those words are promised to every citizen that he shall share in the dignity of man. This dignity cannot be found in a man's possessions. It cannot be found in his power or in his position. It really rests on his right to be treated as a man equal in opportunity to all others. It says that he shall share in freedom. He shall choose his leaders, educate his children, provide for his family according to his ability and his merits as a human being.

To apply any other test, to deny a man his hopes because of his color or race or his religion or the place of his birth is not only to do injustice, it is to deny Americans and to dishonor the dead who gave their lives for American freedom. Our fathers believed that if this noble view of the rights of man was to flourish it must be rooted in democracy. This most basic right of all was the right to choose your own leaders. The history of this country in large measure is the history of expansion of the right to all of our people.

Many of the issues of civil rights are very complex and most difficult. But about this there can and should be no argument: every American citizen must have an equal right to vote. There is no reason which can excuse the denial of that right. There is no duty which weighs more heavily on us than the duty we have to insure that right. Yet the harsh fact is that in many places in this country men and women are kept from voting simply because they are Negroes.

Martin Luther King, Jr. with his wife, Coretta Scott King, lead a black voting rights march from Selma, Alabama, to the state capital in Montgomery.

Every device of which human ingenuity is capable, has been used to deny this right. The Negro citizen may go to register only to be told that the day is wrong, or the hour is late, or the official in charge is absent. And if he persists and, if he manages to present himself to the registrar, he may be disqualified because he did not spell out his middle name, or because he abbreviated a word on the application. And if he manages to fill out an application, he is given a test. The registrar is the sole judge of whether he passes this test. He may be asked to recite the entire Constitution, or explain the most complex provisions of state law.

And even a college degree cannot be used to prove that he can read and write. For the fact is that the only way to pass these barriers is to show a white skin. Experience has clearly shown that the existing process of law cannot overcome systematic and ingenious discrimination. No law that we now have on the books, and I have helped to put three of them there, can insure the right to vote when local officials are determined to deny it. In such a case, our duty must be clear to all of us. The Constitution says that no person shall be kept from voting because of his race or his color.

We have all sworn an oath before God to support and to defend that Constitution. We must now act in obedience to that oath. Wednesday, I will send to Congress a law designed to eliminate illegal barriers to the right to vote. The broad principles of that bill will be in the hands of the Democratic and Republican leaders tomorrow. After they have reviewed it, it will come here formally as a bill. I am grateful for this opportunity to come here tonight at the invitation of the leadership to reason with my friends, to give them my views and to visit with my former colleagues.

I have had prepared a more comprehensive analysis of the legislation which I had intended to transmit to the clerk tomorrow, but which I will submit to the clerks tonight. But I want to really discuss the main proposals of this legislation. This bill will strike down restrictions to voting in all elections, federal, state and local, which have been used to deny Negroes the right to vote.

This bill will establish a simple, uniform standard which cannot be used, however ingenious the effort, to flout our Constitution. It will provide for citizens to be registered by officials of the United States Government, if the state officials refuse to register them. It will eliminate tedious, unnecessary lawsuits which delay the right to vote. Finally, this legislation will insure that properly registered individuals are not prohibited from voting. I will welcome the suggestions from all the members of Congress—I have no doubt that I will get some—on ways and means to strengthen this law and to make it effective.

But experience has plainly shown that this is the only path to carry out the command of the Constitution. To those who seek to avoid action by their national government in their home communities, who want to and who seek to maintain purely local control over elections, the answer is simple: open your polling places to all your people. Allow men and women to register and vote whatever the color of their skin. Extend the rights of citizenship to every citizen of this land. There is no Constitutional issue here. The command of the Constitution is plain. There is no moral issue. It is wrong—deadly wrong—to deny any of your fellow Americans the right to vote in this country.

There is no issue of state's rights or national rights. There is only the struggle for human rights. I have not the slightest doubt what will be your answer. But the last time a President sent a civil rights bill to the Congress it contained a provision to protect voting rights in Federal elections. That civil rights bill was passed after eight long months of debate. And when that bill came to my desk from the Congress for signature, the heart of the voting provision had been eliminated.

This time, on this issue, there must be no delay, or no hesitation, or no compromise with our purpose. We cannot, we must not, refuse to protect the right of every American to vote in every election that he may desire to participate in.

And we ought not, and we cannot, and we must not wait another eight months before we get a bill. We have already waited 100 years and more and the time for waiting is gone. So I ask you to join me in working long hours and nights and weekends, if necessary, to pass this bill. And I don't make that request lightly, for, from the window where I sit, with the problems of our country, I recognize that from outside this chamber is the outraged conscience of a nation, the grave concern of many nations and the harsh judgment of history on our acts.

But even if we pass this bill the battle will not be over. What happened in Selma is part of a far larger movement which reaches into every section and state of America. It is the effort of American Negroes to secure for themselves the full blessings of American life. Their cause must be our cause too. Because it's not just Negroes, but really it's all of us, who must overcome the crippling legacy of bigotry and injustice.

And we shall overcome.

As a man whose roots go deeply into Southern soil, I know how agonizing racial feelings are. I know how difficult it is to reshape the attitudes and the structure of our society. But a century has passed—more than 100 years—since the Negro was freed. And he is not fully free tonight. It was more than 100 years ago that Abraham Lincoln—a great President of another party—signed the Emancipation Proclamation. But emancipation is a proclamation and not a fact.

A century has passed—more than 100 years—since equality was promised, and yet the Negro is not equal. A century has passed since the day of promise, and the promise is unkept. The time of justice has now come, and I tell you that I believe sincerely that no force can hold it back. It is right in the eyes of man and God that it should come, and when it does, I think that day will brighten the lives of every American. For Negroes are not the only victims. How many white children have gone uneducated? How many white families have lived in stark poverty? How many white lives have been scarred by fear, because we wasted energy and our substance to maintain the barriers of hatred and terror?

And so I say to all of you here and to all in the nation tonight that those who appeal to you to hold on to the past do so at the cost of denying you your future. This great rich, restless country can offer opportunity and education and hope to all—all, black and white, North and South, sharecropper and city dweller. These are the enemies: poverty, ignorance, disease. They are our enemies, not our fellow man, not our neighbor.

And these enemies too—poverty, disease and ignorance—we shall overcome.

Now let none of us in any section look with prideful righteousness on the troubles in another section or the problems of our neighbors. There is really no part of America where the promise of equality has been fully kept. In Buffalo as well as in Birmingham, in Philadelphia as well as Selma, Americans are struggling for the fruits of freedom.

This is one nation. What happens in Selma and Cincinnati is a matter of legitimate concern to every American. But let each of us look within our own hearts and our own communities and let each of us put our shoulder to the wheel to root out injustice wherever it exists. As we meet here in this peaceful historic chamber tonight, men from the South, some of whom were at Iwo Jima, men from the North who have carried Old Glory to the far corners of the world and who brought it back without a stain on it, men from the east and from the west are all fighting together without regard to religion or color or region in Vietnam.

A line of policemen on duty in Alabama's state capital, Montgomery, during the black voting rights march led by Dr. Martin Luther King, Jr. from Selma, Alabama.

Men from every region fought for us across the world 20 years ago. And now in these common dangers, in these common sacrifices, the South made its contribution of honor and gallantry no less than any other region in the great republic.

And in some instances, a great many of them, more. And I have not the slightest doubt that good men from everywhere in this country, from the Great Lakes to the Gulf of Mexico, from the Golden Gate to the harbors along the Atlantic, will rally now together in this cause to vindicate the freedom of all Americans. For all of us owe this duty and I believe that all of us will respond to it.

Your president makes that request of every American.

The real hero of this struggle is the American Negro. His actions and protests, his courage to risk safety, and even to risk his life, have awakened the conscience of this nation. His demonstrations have been designed to call attention to injustice, designed to provoke change, designed to stir reform. He has been called upon to make good the promise of America.

And who among us can say that we would have made the same progress were it not for his persistent bravery and his faith in American democracy? For at the real heart of the battle for equality is a deep-seated belief in the democratic process. Equality depends, not on the force of arms or tear gas, but depends upon the force of moral right—not on recourse to violence, but on respect for law and order.

There have been many pressures upon your President and there will be others as the days come and go. But I pledge to you tonight that we intend to fight this battle where it should be fought—in the courts, and in the Congress, and the hearts of men. We must preserve the right of free speech and the right of free assembly. But the right of free speech does not carry with it—as has been said—the right to holler fire in a crowded theatre.

We must preserve the right to free assembly. But free assembly does not carry with it the right to block public thoroughfares to traffic. We do have a right to protest. And a right to march under conditions that do not infringe the Constitutional rights of our neighbors. And I intend to protect all those rights as long as I am permitted to serve in this office.

We will guard against violence, knowing it strikes from our hands the very weapons which we seek—progress, obedience to law, and belief in American values. In Selma, as elsewhere, we seek and pray for peace. We seek order, we seek unity, but we will not accept the peace of stifled rights or the order imposed by fear, or the unity that stifles protest—for peace cannot be purchased at the cost of liberty.

In Selma tonight—and we had a good day there—as in every city we are working for a just and peaceful settlement. We must all remember after this speech I'm making tonight, after the police and the F.B.I. and the Marshals have all gone, and after you have promptly passed this bill, the people of Selma and the other cities of the nation must still live and work together.

And when the attention of the nation has gone elsewhere they must try to heal the wounds and to build a new community. This cannot be easily done on a battleground of violence as the history of the South itself shows. It is in recognition of this that men of both races have shown such an outstandingly impressive responsibility in recent days—last Tuesday and again today.

The bill I am presenting to you will be known as a civil rights bill. But in a larger sense, most of the program I am recommending is a civil rights program. Its object is to open the city of hope to all people of all races, because all Americans just must have the right to vote, and we are going to give them that right.

All Americans must have the privileges of citizenship, regardless of race, and they are going to have those privileges of citizenship regardless of race.

But I would like to caution you and remind you that to exercise these privileges takes much more than just legal rights. It requires a trained mind and a healthy body. It requires a decent home and the chance to find a job and the opportunity to escape from the clutches of poverty.

Of course people cannot contribute to the nation if they are never taught to read or write; if their bodies are stunted from hunger; if their sickness goes untended; if their life is spent in hopeless poverty, just drawing a welfare check.

So we want to open the gates to opportunity. But we're also going to give all our people, black and white, the help that they need to walk through those gates. My first job after college was as a teacher in Cotulla, Texas, in a small Mexican-American school. Few of them could speak English and I couldn't speak much Spanish. My students were poor and they often came to class without breakfast and hungry. And they knew even in their youth the pain of prejudice. They never seemed to know why people disliked them, but they knew it was so because I saw it in their eyes.

I often walked home late in the afternoon after the classes were finished wishing there was more that I could do. But all I knew was to teach them the little that I knew, hoping that I might help them against the hardships that lay ahead. And somehow you never forget what poverty and hatred can do when you see its scars on the hopeful face of a young child.

I never thought then, in 1928, that I would be standing here in 1965. It never even occurred to me in my fondest dreams that I might have the chance to help the sons and daughters of those

A group of voters lining up outside the polling station in Peachtree, Alabama, in 1966, a year after the Voting Rights Act was passed.

students, and to help people like them all over this country. But now I do have that chance. And I'll let you in on a secret—I mean to use it. And I hope that you will use it with me.

This is the richest, most powerful country which ever occupied this globe. The might of past empires is little compared to ours. But I do not want to be the president who built empires, or sought grandeur, or extended dominion.

I want to be the president who educated young children to the wonders of their world. I want to be the President who helped to feed the hungry and to prepare them to be taxpayers instead of tax eaters. I want to be the President who helped the poor to find their own way and who protected the right of every citizen to vote in every election. I want to be the President who helped to end hatred among his fellow men and who promoted love among the people of all races, all regions and all parties. I want to be the President who helped to end war among the brothers of this earth.

And so, at the request of your beloved Speaker and the Senator from Montana, the Majority Leader, the Senator from Illinois, the Minority Leader, Mr. McCullock and other members of both parties, I came here tonight, not as President Roosevelt came down one time in person to veto a bonus bill; not as President Truman came down one time to urge passage of a railroad bill, but I came down here to ask you to share this task with me. And to share it with the people that we both work for.

I want this to be the Congress—Republicans and Democrats alike—which did all these things for all these people. Beyond this great chamber—out yonder—in fifty states are the people that we serve. Who can tell what deep and unspoken hopes are in their hearts tonight as they sit there and listen? We all can guess, from our own lives, how difficult they often find their own pursuit of happiness, how many problems each little family has. They look most of all to themselves for their future, but I think that they also look to each of us.

Above the pyramid on the Great Seal of the United States it says in Latin, "God has favored our undertaking." God will not favor everything that we do. It is rather our duty to divine His will. But I cannot help but believe that He truly understands and that He really favors the undertaking that we begin here tonight.

On August 6, 1965 President Johnson signed the Voting Rights Act ending the practice of administering literacy, knowledge or other tests that had been used to keep African-Americans from registering to vote.

"I Shall Not Seek, and
I Will Not Accept"

President Lyndon B. Johnson, March 31, 1968

On March 31, 1968, President Lyndon B. Johnson stunned the world with his surprise announcement that he would not seek re-election.

The announcement came at the end of this TV speech concerning the situation in Vietnam, where increasing numbers of young Americans were being killed amid the recent escalation of the war.

In January of 1968, the Tet offensive occurred, in which North Vietnamese troops attacked 36 provincial capitals and 5 major cities in South Vietnam, including an attack on the U.S. embassy in Saigon and the presidential palace.

Filmed footage of the offensive and its resulting carnage appeared on nightly news programs seen by the American public. Unlike previous wars, news personnel were not censored and thus often took graphic front line combat footage.

Year after year of TV news reports showing bloodied young Americans and dead Vietnamese civilians eventually led many to question the necessity of the entire ordeal. By 1968, demonstrations and unrest had erupted on college campuses with demands for an immediate end to the war.

Vietnam veterans, reservists and other activists in a 1968 protest for an end to the war in Vietnam.

Amid the mounting death toll and continuing erosion of popular and political support for the war, President Johnson was faced with having to decide America's future course in the conflict. His choices included possible escalation in an effort to win the war, or the pursuit of peace with an enemy who now seemed determined to fight and win no matter what the cost.

Good evening, my fellow Americans: Tonight I want to speak to you of peace in Vietnam and Southeast Asia. No other question so preoccupies our people. No other dream so absorbs the 250 million human beings who live in that part of the world. No other goal motivates American policy in Southeast Asia.

For years, representatives of our Government and others have traveled the world—seeking to find a basis for peace talks.

Since last September, they have carried the offer that I made public at San Antonio. That offer was this:

That the United States would stop its bombardment of North Vietnam when that would lead promptly to productive discussions—and that we would assume that North Vietnam would not take military advantage of our restraint.

Hanoi denounced this offer, both privately and publicly. Even while the search for peace was going on, North Vietnam rushed their preparations for a savage assault on the people, the government, and the allies of South Vietnam.

Their attack—during the Tet holidays—failed to achieve its principal objectives.

It did not collapse the elected government of South Vietnam or shatter its army—as the Communists had hoped.

It did not produce a "general uprising" among the people of the cities as they had predicted.

The Communists were unable to maintain control of any of the more than 30 cities that they attacked. And they took very heavy casualties.

But they did compel the South Vietnamese and their allies to move certain forces from the countryside into the cities.

They caused widespread disruption and suffering. Their attacks, and the battles that followed, made refugees of half a million human beings.

The Communists may renew their attack any day.

They are, it appears, trying to make 1968 the year of decision in South Vietnam—the year that brings, if not final victory or defeat, at least a turning point in the struggle.

This much is clear: If they do mount another round of heavy attacks, they will not succeed in destroying the fighting power of South Vietnam and its allies.

But tragically, this is also clear: Many men—on both sides of the struggle—will be lost. A nation that has already suffered 20 years of warfare will suffer once again. Armies on both sides will take new casualties. And the war will go on.

There is no need for this to be so.

There is no need to delay the talks that could bring an end to this long and this bloody war.

Tonight, I renew the offer I made last August—to stop the bombardment of North Vietnam. We ask that talks begin promptly, that they be serious talks on the substance of peace. We assume that during those talks Hanoi will not take advantage of our restraint.

Tombstones of soldiers at Arlington cemetery.

We are prepared to move immediately toward peace through negotiations.

So, tonight, in the hope that this action will lead to early talks, I am taking the first step to deescalate the conflict. We are reducing—substantially reducing—the present level of hostilities.

And we are doing so unilaterally, and at once.

Tonight, I have ordered our aircraft and our naval vessels to make no attacks on North Vietnam, except in the area north of the demilitarized zone where the continuing enemy buildup directly threatens allied forward positions and where the movements of their troops and supplies are clearly related to that threat.

The area in which we are stopping our attacks includes almost 90 percent of North Vietnam's population, and most of its territory. Thus there will be no attacks around the principal populated areas, or in the food-producing areas of North Vietnam.

Even this very limited bombing of the North could come to an early end—if our restraint is matched by restraint in Hanoi. But I cannot in good conscience stop all bombing so long as to do so would immediately and directly endanger the lives of our men and our allies. Whether a complete bombing halt becomes possible in the future will be determined by events.

Our purpose in this action is to bring about a reduction in the level of violence that now exists.

It is to save the lives of brave men—and to save the lives of innocent women and children. It is to permit the contending forces to move closer to a political settlement.

And tonight, I call upon the United Kingdom and I call upon the Soviet Union—as cochairmen of the Geneva Conferences, and as permanent members of the United Nations Security Council—to do all they can to move from the unilateral act of deescalation that I have just announced toward genuine peace in Southeast Asia.

A soldier in the sunset.

Now, as in the past, the United States is ready to send its representatives to any forum, at any time, to discuss the means of bringing this ugly war to an end.

I am designating one of our most distinguished Americans, Ambassador Averell Harriman, as my personal representative for such talks. In addition, I have asked Ambassador Llewellyn Thompson, who returned from Moscow for consultation, to be available to join Ambassador Harriman at Geneva or any other suitable place—just as soon as Hanoi agrees to a conference.

I call upon President Ho Chi Minh to respond positively, and favorably, to this new step toward peace.

But if peace does not come now through negotiations, it will come when Hanoi understands that our common resolve is unshakable, and our common strength is invincible.

Tonight, we and the other allied nations are contributing 600,000 fighting men to assist 700,000 South Vietnamese troops in defending their little country.

Our presence there has always rested on this basic belief: The main burden of preserving their freedom must be carried out by them—by the South Vietnamese themselves.

We and our allies can only help to provide a shield behind which the people of South Vietnam can survive and can grow and develop. On their efforts—on their determination and resourcefulness—the outcome will ultimately depend.

That small, beleaguered nation has suffered terrible punishment for more than 20 years.

I pay tribute once again tonight to the great courage and endurance of its people. South Vietnam supports armed forces tonight of almost 700,000 men—and I call your attention to the fact that this is the equivalent of more than 10 million in our own population. Its people maintain their firm determination to be free of domination by the North.

There has been substantial progress, I think, in building a durable government during these last 3 years. The South Vietnam of 1965 could not have survived the enemy's Tet offensive of 1968. The elected government of South Vietnam survived that attack—and is rapidly repairing the devastation that it wrought.

The South Vietnamese know that further efforts are going to be required:

- to expand their own armed forces,

- to move back into the countryside as quickly as possible,

- to increase their taxes,

- to select the very best men that they have for civil and military responsibility,

- to achieve a new unity within their constitutional government, and

- to include in the national effort all those groups who wish to preserve South Vietnam's control over its own destiny.

Last week President Thieu ordered the mobilization of 135,000 additional South Vietnamese. He plans to reach—as soon as possible—a total military strength of more than 800,000 men.

To achieve this, the Government of South Vietnam started the drafting of 19-year-olds on March 1st. On May 1st, the Government will begin the drafting of 18-year-olds.

Last month, 10,000 men volunteered for military service—that was two and a half times the number of volunteers during the same month last year. Since the middle of January, more than 48,000 South Vietnamese have joined the armed forces—and nearly half of them volunteered to do so.

All men in the South Vietnamese armed forces have had their tours of duty extended for the duration of the war, and reserves are now being called up for immediate active duty.

President Thieu told his people last week:

"We must make greater efforts and accept more sacrifices because, as I have said many times, this is our country. The existence of our nation is at stake, and this is mainly a Vietnamese responsibility."

He warned his people that a major national effort is required to root out corruption and incompetence at all levels of government.

We applaud this evidence of determination on the part of South Vietnam. Our first priority will be to support their effort.

We shall accelerate the reequipment of South Vietnam's armed forces—in order to meet the enemy's increased firepower. This will enable them progressively to undertake a larger share of combat operations against the Communist invaders.

On many occasions I have told the American people that we would send to Vietnam those forces that are required to accomplish our mission there. So, with that as our guide, we have previously authorized a force level of approximately 525,000.

Some weeks ago—to help meet the enemy's new offensive—we sent to Vietnam about 11,000 additional Marine and airborne troops. They were deployed by air in 48 hours, on an emergency basis. But the artillery, tank, aircraft, medical, and other units that were needed to work with and to support these infantry troops in combat could not then accompany them by air on that short notice.

In order that these forces may reach maximum combat effectiveness, the Joint Chiefs of Staff have recommended to me that we should prepare to send—during the next 5 months—support troops totaling approximately 13,500 men.

A portion of these men will be made available from our active forces. The balance will come from reserve component units which will be called up for service.

The actions that we have taken since the beginning of the year:

- to reequip the South Vietnamese forces,

- to meet our responsibilities in Korea, as well as our responsibilities in Vietnam,

- to meet price increases and the cost of activating and deploying reserve forces,

- to replace helicopters and provide the other military supplies we need, all of these actions are going to require additional expenditures.

The tentative estimate of those additional expenditures is $2.5 billion in this fiscal year, and $2.6 billion in the next fiscal year.

These projected increases in expenditures for our national security will bring into sharper focus the Nation's need for immediate action: action to protect the prosperity of the American people and to protect the strength and the stability of our American dollar.

On many occasions I have pointed out that, without a tax bill or decreased expenditures, next year's deficit would again be around $20 billion. I have emphasized the need to set strict priorities in our spending. I have stressed that failure to act and to act promptly and decisively would raise very strong doubts throughout the world about America's willingness to keep its financial house in order.

Yet Congress has not acted. And tonight we face the sharpest financial threat in the postwar era—a threat to the dollar's role as the keystone of international trade and finance in the world.

Last week, at the monetary conference in Stockholm, the major industrial countries decided to take a big step toward creating a new international monetary asset that will strengthen the international monetary system. I am very proud of the very able work done by Secretary Fowler and Chairman Martin of the Federal Reserve Board.

But to make this system work the United States just must bring its balance of payments to—or very close to—equilibrium. We must have a responsible fiscal policy in this country. The passage of a tax bill now, together with expenditure control that the Congress may desire and dictate, is absolutely necessary to protect this Nation's security, to continue our prosperity, and to meet the needs of our people.

What is at stake is 7 years of unparalleled prosperity. In those 7 years, the real income of the average American, after taxes, rose by almost 30 percent—a gain as large as that of the entire preceding 19 years.

So the steps that we must take to convince the world are exactly the steps we must take to sustain our own economic strength here at home. In the past 8 months, prices and interest rates have risen because of our inaction.

We must, therefore, now do everything we can to move from debate to action—from talking to voting. There is, I believe—I hope there is—in both Houses of the Congress—a growing sense of urgency that this situation just must be acted upon and must be corrected.

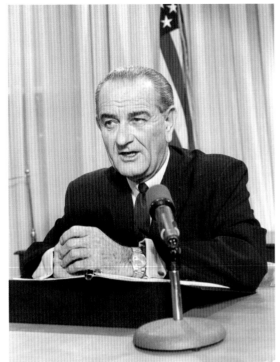

U.S. President Lyndon Baines Johnson appeals to Communist Vietnamese leader Ho Chi Minh on March 31, 1968 for peace in Vietnam and announces he will not seek re-election in a televised speech, Washington, DC.

My budget in January was, we thought, a tight one. It fully reflected our evaluation of most of the demanding needs of this Nation.

But in these budgetary matters, the President does not decide alone. The Congress has the power and the duty to determine appropriations and taxes.

The Congress is now considering our proposals and they are considering reductions in the budget that we submitted.

As part of a program of fiscal restraint that includes the tax surcharge, I shall approve appropriate reductions in the January budget when and if Congress so decides that that should be done.

One thing is unmistakably clear, however: Our deficit just must be reduced. Failure to act could bring on conditions that would strike hardest at those people that all of us are trying so hard to help.

These times call for prudence in this land of plenty. I believe that we have the character to provide it, and tonight I plead with the Congress and with the people to act promptly to serve the national interest, and thereby serve all of our people.

Now let me give you my estimate of the chances for peace:

- the peace that will one day stop the bloodshed in South Vietnam,

- that will permit all the Vietnamese people to rebuild and develop their land,

- that will permit us to turn more fully to our own tasks here at home.

I cannot promise that the initiative that I have announced tonight will be completely successful in achieving peace any more than the 30 others that we have undertaken and agreed to in recent years.

But it is our fervent hope that North Vietnam, after years of fighting that have left the issue unresolved, will now cease its efforts to achieve a military victory and will join with us in moving toward the peace table.

And there may come a time when South Vietnamese—on both sides—are able to work out a way to settle their own differences by free political choice rather than by war.

As Hanoi considers its course, it should be in no doubt of our intentions. It must not miscalculate the pressures within our democracy in this election year.

We have no intention of widening this war.

But the United States will never accept a fake solution to this long and arduous struggle and call it peace.

No one can foretell the precise terms of an eventual settlement.

Our objective in South Vietnam has never been the annihilation of the enemy. It has been to bring about a recognition in Hanoi that its objective—taking over the South by force—could not be achieved.

We think that peace can be based on the Geneva Accords of 1954—under political conditions that permit the South Vietnamese—all the South Vietnamese—to chart their course free of any outside domination or interference, from us or from anyone else.

So tonight I reaffirm the pledge that we made at Manila—that we are prepared to withdraw our forces from South Vietnam as the other side withdraws its forces to the north, stops the infiltration, and the level of violence thus subsides.

Our goal of peace and self-determination in Vietnam is directly related to the future of all of Southeast Asia—where much has happened to inspire confidence during the past 10 years. We have done all that we knew how to do to contribute and to help build that confidence.

A number of its nations have shown what can be accomplished under conditions of security. Since 1966, Indonesia, the fifth largest nation in all the world, with a population of more than 100 million people, has had a government that is dedicated to peace with its neighbors and improved conditions for its own people. Political and economic cooperation between nations has grown rapidly.

Visitors at the Vietnam Memorial Wall

I think every American can take a great deal of pride in the role that we have played in bringing this about in Southeast Asia. We can rightly judge—as responsible Southeast Asians themselves do—that the progress of the past 3 years would have been far less likely—if not completely impossible—if America's sons and others had not made their stand in Vietnam.

At Johns Hopkins University, about 3 years ago, I announced that the United States would take part in the great work of developing Southeast Asia, including the Mekong Valley, for all the people of that region. Our determination to help build a better land—a better land for men on both sides of the present conflict—has not diminished in the least. Indeed, the ravages of war, I think, have made it more urgent than ever.

So, I repeat on behalf of the United States again tonight what I said at Johns Hopkins—that North Vietnam could take its place in this common effort just as soon as peace comes.

Over time, a wider framework of peace and security in Southeast Asia may become possible. The new cooperation of the nations of the area could be a foundation-stone. Certainly friendship with the nations of such a Southeast Asia is what the United States seeks—and that is all that the United States seeks.

One day, my fellow citizens, there will be peace in Southeast Asia.

It will come because the people of Southeast Asia want it—those whose armies are at war tonight, and those who, though threatened, have thus far been spared.

Peace will come because Asians were willing to work for it—and to sacrifice for it—and to die by the thousands for it.

But let it never be forgotten: Peace will come also because America sent her sons to help secure it.

It has not been easy—far from it. During the past 4 years, it has been my fate and my responsibility to be Commander in Chief. I have lived—daily and nightly—with the cost of this war. I know the pain that it has inflicted. I know, perhaps better than anyone, the misgivings that it has aroused.

Throughout this entire, long period, I have been sustained by a single principle: that what we are doing now, in Vietnam, is vital not only to the security of Southeast Asia, but it is vital to the security of every American.

Surely we have treaties which we must respect. Surely we have commitments that we are going to keep. Resolutions of the Congress testify to the need to resist aggression in the world and in Southeast Asia.

But the heart of our involvement in South Vietnam—under three different presidents, three separate administrations—has always been America's own security.

And the larger purpose of our involvement has always been to help the nations of Southeast Asia become independent and stand alone, self-sustaining, as members of a great world community—at peace with themselves, and at peace with all others.

With such an Asia, our country—and the world—will be far more secure than it is tonight.

I believe that a peaceful Asia is far nearer to reality because of what America has done in Vietnam. I believe that the men who endure the dangers of battle—fighting there for us tonight—are helping the entire world avoid far greater conflicts, far wider wars, far more destruction, than this one.

The peace that will bring them home someday will come. Tonight I have offered the first in what I hope will be a series of mutual moves toward peace.

I pray that it will not be rejected by the leaders of North Vietnam. I pray that they will accept it as a means by which the sacrifices of their own people may be ended. And I ask your help and your support, my fellow citizens, for this effort to reach across the battlefield toward an early peace.

Finally, my fellow Americans, let me say this:

Of those to whom much is given, much is asked. I cannot say and no man could say that no more will be asked of us.

Yet, I believe that now, no less than when the decade began, this generation of Americans is willing to "pay any price, bear any burden, meet any hardship, support any friend, oppose any foe to assure the survival and the success of liberty."

An officer pays his respects at The Wall.

Since those words were spoken by John F. Kennedy, the people of America have kept that compact with mankind's noblest cause.

And we shall continue to keep it.

Yet, I believe that we must always be mindful of this one thing, whatever the trials and the tests ahead. The ultimate strength of our country and our cause will lie not in powerful weapons or infinite resources or boundless wealth, but will lie in the unity of our people.

This I believe very deeply.

Throughout my entire public career I have followed the personal philosophy that I am a free man, an American, a public servant, and a member of my party, in that order always and only.

For 37 years in the service of our Nation, first as a Congressman, as a Senator, and as Vice President, and now as your President, I have put the unity of the people first. I have put it ahead of any divisive partisanship.

And in these times as in times before, it is true that a house divided against itself by the spirit of faction, of party, of region, of religion, of race, is a house that cannot stand.

There is division in the American house now. There is divisiveness among us all tonight. And holding the trust that is mine, as President of all the people, I cannot disregard the peril to the progress of the American people and the hope and the prospect of peace for all peoples.

So, I would ask all Americans, whatever their personal interests or concern, to guard against divisiveness and all its ugly consequences.

Fifty-two months and 10 days ago, in a moment of tragedy and trauma, the duties of this office fell upon me. I asked then for your help and God's, that we might continue America on its course, binding up our wounds, healing our history, moving forward in new unity, to clear the American agenda and to keep the American commitment for all of our people.

United we have kept that commitment. United we have enlarged that commitment.

Through all time to come, I think America will be a stronger nation, a more just society, and a land of greater opportunity and fulfillment because of what we have all done together in these years of unparalleled achievement.

Our reward will come in the life of freedom, peace, and hope that our children will enjoy through ages ahead.

What we won when all of our people united just must not now be lost in suspicion, distrust, selfishness, and politics among any of our people.

Believing this as I do, I have concluded that I should not permit the Presidency to become involved in the partisan divisions that are developing in this political year.

With America's sons in the fields far away, with America's future under challenge right here at home, with our hopes and the world's hopes for peace in the balance every day, I do not believe that I should devote an hour or a day of my time to any personal partisan causes or to any duties other than the awesome duties of this office—the Presidency of your country.

Accordingly, I shall not seek, and I will not accept, the nomination of my party for another term as your President.

But let men everywhere know, however, that a strong, a confident, and a vigilant America stands ready tonight to seek an honorable peace—and stands ready tonight to defend an honored cause—whatever the price, whatever the burden, whatever the sacrifice that duty may require.

Thank you for listening.

Good night and God bless all of you.

"One Giant Leap for Mankind"

Neil Armstrong, July 20, 1969

Left to right, Neil Armstrong, Michael Collins, and Edwin "Buzz" Aldrin, Jr., of the Apollo 11 moon landing mission, hold a conversation with President Richard Nixon through the window of their Mobile Quarantine Facility. The crew was undergoing a two-week period of quarantine following their return to earth on July 24th, 1969.

"That's one small step for man, one giant leap for mankind."

These words, transmitted from the moon on July 20, 1969, are what people on earth heard and printed in newspapers all over the world. They were spoken by the first man to set foot on the moon, Apollo 11 Mission Commander Neil Armstrong. What he meant to say, and thought he'd said, as he took that momentous first step out of the Eagle moon-landing module, was "That's one small step for a man, one giant leap for mankind." NASA communication reviews reveal this small verbal sound was obscured in the static of transmission.

WAR POWERS RESOLUTION

November 7, 1973

Excerpted:

War Powers Resolution, November 7, 1973

Public Law 93-148, 93rd Congress, H. J. Res. 542

The War Powers Resolution was passed by Congress in the wake of the Vietnam conflict—so protracted and costly, not only in dollars but in esteem, human life, and dignity. It was clear that the United States had become entangled in the Vietnam situation through a chain of events having to do with foreign policy, and that entry into those hostilities had not been fully considered by guidelines present in our Constitution.

Joint Resolution Concerning the war powers of Congress and the President.

Resolved by the Senate and the House of Representatives of the United States of America in Congress assembled,

SHORT TITLE

SECTION 1.

This joint resolution may be cited as the "War Powers Resolution."

PURPOSE AND POLICY

SEC. 2.

(a) It is the purpose of this joint resolution to fulfill the intent of the framers of the Constitution of the United States and insure that the collective judgment of both the Congress

Soldiers in full dress standing at attention, West Point Military Academy.

and the President will apply to the introduction of United States Armed Forces into hostilities, or into situations where imminent involvement in hostilities is clearly indicated by the circumstances, and to the continued use of such forces in hostilities or in such situations.

(b) Under article I, section 8, of the Constitution, it is specifically provided that the Congress shall have the power to make all laws necessary and proper for carrying into execution, not only its own powers but also all other powers vested by the Constitution in the Government of the United States, or in any department or officer thereof.

(c) The constitutional powers of the President as Commander-in-Chief to introduce United States Armed Forces into hostilities, or into situations where imminent involvement in hostilities is clearly indicated by the circumstances, are exercised only pursuant to (1) a declaration of war, (2) specific statutory authorization, or (3) a national emergency created by attack upon the United States, its territories or possessions, or its armed forces.

Midshipmen at the U.S. Naval Academy, Annapolis, marching in formation.

The Resolution goes on to clarify how, in the absence of a declaration of war or direct attack on our country, the President is to consult with Congress in every instance before introducing United States Armed Forces into hostilities or into any situation where imminent involvement in hostilities is clearly indicated by the circumstances.

It further sets out all parameters of how, if Congress is in agreement and forces are introduced, the president shall regularly confer with Congress until United States Armed Forces are no longer engaged in hostilities or have been removed from such situations.

Prescriptions are made for the procedures, priorities, and time limits that are to be observed in moving any requests or resolves through the judicial process, and the Resolution concludes:

SEPARABILITY CLAUSE

SEC. 9.

If any provision of this joint resolution or the application thereof to any person or circumstance is held invalid, the remainder of the joint resolution and the application of such provision to any other person or circumstance shall not be affected thereby.

EFFECTIVE DATE

SEC. 10.

This joint resolution shall take effect on the date of its enactment.

SHOW THE FLAG

By Edgar Albert Guest

Show the flag and let it wave
As a symbol of the brave;
Let it float upon the breeze
As a sign for each who sees
That beneath it, where it rides,
Loyalty to-day abides.

Show the flag and signify
That it wasn't born to die;
Let its colors speak for you
That you still are standing true,
True in sight of God and man
To the work that flag began.

Show the flag that all may see
That you serve humanity.
Let it whisper to the breeze

That comes singing through the trees
That whatever storms descend
You'll be faithful to the end.

Show the flag and let it fly,
Cheering every passer-by.
Men that may have stepped aside,
May have lost their old-time pride,
May behold it there, and then,
Consecrate themselves again.

Show the flag! The day is gone
When men blindly hurry on
Serving only gods of gold;
Now the spirit that was cold
Warms again to courage fine.
Show the flag and fall in line!

"Awakened to Danger and Called to Defend Freedom"

President George W. Bush's Address to Congress, September 20, 2001

Mr. Speaker, Mr. President pro tem, members of Congress and fellow Americans:

In the normal course of events, presidents come to this chamber to report on the state of the union. Tonight, no such report is needed. It has already been delivered by the American people.

We have seen it in the courage of passengers who rushed terrorists to save others on the ground. Passengers like an exceptional man named Todd Beamer. And would you please help me welcome his wife, Lisa Beamer, here tonight.

We have seen the state of our union in the endurance of rescuers working past exhaustion. We've seen the unfurling of flags, the lighting of candles, the giving of blood, the saying of prayers in English, Hebrew and Arabic. We have seen the decency of a loving and giving people who have made the grief of strangers their own.

My fellow citizens, for the last nine days, the entire world has seen for itself the state of our union, and it is strong.

Tonight we are a country awakened to danger and called to defend freedom. Our grief has turned to anger and anger to resolution. Whether we bring our enemies to justice or bring justice to our enemies, justice will be done.

President George W. Bush at the White House in Washington, October 2001.

(photo by Mark Wilson/Getty Images.)

I thank the Congress for its leadership at such an important time. All of America was touched on the evening of the tragedy to see Republicans and Democrats joined together on the steps of this Capitol singing "God Bless America." And you did more than sing. You acted by delivering $40 billion to rebuild our communities and meet the needs of our military.

Speaker Hastert, Minority Leader Gephardt, Majority Leader Daschle and Senator Lott, I thank you for your friendship, for your leadership and for your service to our country.

And on behalf of the American people, I thank the world for its outpouring of support. America will never forget the sounds of our national anthem playing at Buckingham Palace, on the streets of Paris and at Berlin's Brandenburg Gate. We will not forget South Korean children gathering to pray outside our embassy in Seoul or the prayers of sympathy offered at a mosque in Cairo. We will not forget moments of silence and days of mourning in Australia and Africa and Latin America.

Nor will we forget the citizens of 80 other nations who died with our own: dozens of Pakistanis, more than 130 Israelis, more than 250 citizens of India, men and women from El Salvador, Iran, Mexico and Japan, and hundreds of British citizens.

America has no truer friend than Great Britain.

Once again we are joined together in a great cause. I'm so honored the British prime minister has crossed an ocean to show his unity with America. Thank you for coming, friend.

On September 11, enemies of freedom committed an act of war against our country. Americans have known wars. But for the past 136 years they have been wars on foreign soil, except for one Sunday in 1941. Americans have known the casualties of war. But not at the center of a great city on a peaceful morning. Americans have known surprise attacks. But never before on thousands of civilians. All of this was brought upon us in a single day. And night fell on a different world, a world where freedom itself is under attack.

Americans have many questions tonight. Americans are asking: Who attacked our country? The evidence we have gathered all points to a collection of loosely affiliated terrorist organizations known as al Qaeda. They are the same murderers indicted for bombing American embassies in Tanzania and Kenya, and responsible for bombing the USS Cole.

Al Qaeda is to terror what the mafia is to crime. But its goal is not making money; its goal is remaking the world — and imposing its radical beliefs on people everywhere.

The terrorists practice a fringe form of Islamic extremism that has been rejected by Muslim scholars and the vast majority of Muslim clerics — a fringe movement that perverts the peaceful teachings of Islam. The terrorists' directive commands them to kill Christians and Jews, to kill all Americans, and make no distinction among military and civilians, including women and children.

This group and its leader — a person named Osama bin Laden — are linked to many other organizations in different countries, including the Egyptian Islamic Jihad and the Islamic Movement of Uzbekistan. There are thousands of these terrorists in more than 60 countries. They are recruited from their own nations and neighborhoods and brought to camps in places like Afghanistan, where they are trained in the tactics of terror. They are sent back to their homes or sent to hide in countries around the world to plot evil and destruction.

The leadership of al Qaeda has great influence in Afghanistan and supports the Taliban regime in controlling most of that country. In Afghanistan, we see al Qaeda's vision for the world.

Afghanistan's people have been brutalized — many are starving and many have fled. Women are not allowed to attend school. You can be jailed for owning a television. Religion can be practiced only as their leaders dictate. A man can be jailed in Afghanistan if his beard is not long enough.

The United States respects the people of Afghanistan — after all, we are currently its largest source of humanitarian aid — but we condemn the Taliban regime. (Applause.) It is not only repressing its own people, it is threatening people everywhere by sponsoring and sheltering and supplying terrorists. By aiding and abetting murder, the Taliban regime is committing murder.

And tonight, the United States of America makes the following demands on the Taliban: Deliver to United States authorities all the leaders of al Qaeda who hide in your land. (Applause.) Release all foreign nationals, including American citizens, you have unjustly imprisoned. Protect foreign journalists, diplomats and aid workers in your country. Close immediately and permanently every terrorist training camp in Afghanistan, and hand over every terrorist, and every person in their support structure, to appropriate authorities. (Applause.) Give the United States full access to terrorist training camps, so we can make sure they are no longer operating.

These demands are not open to negotiation or discussion. (Applause.) The Taliban must act, and act immediately. They will hand over the terrorists, or they will share in their fate.

I also want to speak tonight directly to Muslims throughout the world. We respect your faith. It's practiced freely by many millions of Americans, and by millions more in countries that America counts as friends. Its teachings are good and peaceful, and those who commit evil in the name of Allah blaspheme the name of Allah. (Applause.) The terrorists are traitors to their own faith, trying, in effect, to hijack Islam itself. The enemy of America is not our many Muslim friends; it is not our many Arab friends. Our enemy is a radical network of terrorists, and every government that supports them. (Applause.)

President George W. Bush flanked by Secretary of State Colin Powell, in Washington, October 4, 2001. **(Photo by Mark Wilson/Getty Images.)**

Our war on terror begins with al Qaeda, but it does not end there. It will not end until every terrorist group of global reach has been found, stopped and defeated. (Applause.)

Americans are asking, why do they hate us? They hate what we see right here in this chamber — a democratically elected government. Their leaders are self-appointed. They hate our freedoms — our freedom of religion, our freedom of speech, our freedom to vote and assemble and disagree with each other.

They want to overthrow existing governments in many Muslim countries, such as Egypt, Saudi

Arabia, and Jordan. They want to drive Israel out of the Middle East. They want to drive Christians and Jews out of vast regions of Asia and Africa.

These terrorists kill not merely to end lives, but to disrupt and end a way of life. With every atrocity, they hope that America grows fearful, retreating from the world and forsaking our friends. They stand against us, because we stand in their way.

We are not deceived by their pretenses to piety. We have seen their kind before. They are the heirs of all the murderous ideologies of the 20th century. By sacrificing human life to serve their radical visions — by abandoning every value except the will to power — they follow in the path of fascism, and Nazism, and totalitarianism. And they will follow that path all the way, to where it ends: in history's unmarked grave of discarded lies. (Applause.)

Americans are asking: How will we fight and win this war? We will direct every resource at our command — every means of diplomacy, every tool of intelligence, every instrument of law enforcement, every financial influence, and every necessary weapon of war — to the disruption and to the defeat of the global terror network.

This war will not be like the war against Iraq a decade ago, with a decisive liberation of territory and a swift conclusion. It will not look like the air war above Kosovo two years ago, where no ground troops were used and not a single American was lost in combat.

Our response involves far more than instant retaliation and isolated strikes. Americans should not expect one battle, but a lengthy campaign, unlike any other we have ever seen. It may include dramatic strikes, visible on TV, and covert operations, secret even in success. We will starve terrorists of funding, turn them one against another, drive them from place to place, until there is no refuge or no rest. And we will pursue nations that provide aid or safe haven to terrorism. Every nation, in every region, now has a decision to make. Either you are with us, or you are with the terrorists. (Applause.) From this day forward, any nation that continues to harbor or support terrorism will be regarded by the United States as a hostile regime.

Our nation has been put on notice: We are not immune from attack. We will take defensive measures against terrorism to protect Americans. Today, dozens of federal departments and agencies, as well as state and local governments, have responsibilities affecting homeland security. These efforts must be coordinated at the highest level. So tonight I announce the creation of a Cabinet-level position reporting directly to me — the Office of Homeland Security.

And tonight I also announce a distinguished American to lead this effort, to strengthen American security: a military veteran, an effective governor, a true patriot, a trusted friend — Pennsylvania's Tom Ridge. (Applause.) He will lead, oversee and coordinate a comprehensive national strategy to safeguard our country against terrorism, and respond to any attacks that may come.

These measures are essential. But the only way to defeat terrorism as a threat to our way of life is to stop it, eliminate it, and destroy it where it grows. (Applause.)

Many will be involved in this effort, from FBI agents to intelligence operatives to the reservists we have called to active duty. All deserve our thanks, and all have our prayers. And tonight, a few miles from the damaged Pentagon, I have a message for our military: Be ready. I've called the Armed Forces to alert, and there is a reason. The hour is coming when America will act, and you will make us proud. (Applause.)

This is not, however, just America's fight. And what is at stake is not just America's freedom. This is the world's fight. This is civilization's fight. This is the fight of all who believe in progress and pluralism, tolerance and freedom.

We ask every nation to join us. We will ask, and we will need, the help of police forces, intelligence services, and banking systems around the world. The United States is grateful that many nations and many international organizations have already responded — with sympathy and with support. Nations from Latin America, to Asia, to Africa, to Europe, to the Islamic world. Perhaps the NATO Charter reflects best the attitude of the world: An attack on one is an attack on all.

The civilized world is rallying to America's side. They understand that if this terror goes unpunished, their own cities, their own citizens may be next. Terror, unanswered, can not only bring down buildings, it can threaten the stability of legitimate governments. And you know what — we're not going to allow it. (Applause.)

Americans are asking: What is expected of us? I ask you to live your lives, and hug your children. I know many citizens have fears tonight, and I ask you to be calm and resolute, even in the face of a continuing threat.

I ask you to uphold the values of America, and remember why so many have come here. We are in a fight for our principles, and our first responsibility is to live by them. No one should be singled out for unfair treatment or unkind words because of their ethnic background or religious faith. (Applause.)

I ask you to continue to support the victims of this tragedy with your contributions. Those who want to give can go to a central source of information, libertyunites.org, to find the names of groups providing direct help in New York, Pennsylvania, and Virginia.

The thousands of FBI agents who are now at work in this investigation may need your cooperation, and I ask you to give it.

I ask for your patience, with the delays and inconveniences that may accompany tighter security; and for your patience in what will be a long struggle.

I ask your continued participation and confidence in the American economy. Terrorists attacked a symbol of American prosperity. They did not touch its source. America is successful because of the hard work, and creativity, and enterprise of our people. These were the true strengths of our economy before September 11th, and they are our strengths today. (Applause.)

And, finally, please continue praying for the victims of terror and their families, for those in

A battleship during a ceremony.

uniform, and for our great country. Prayer has comforted us in sorrow, and will help strengthen us for the journey ahead.

Tonight I thank my fellow Americans for what you have already done and for what you will do. And ladies and gentlemen of the Congress, I thank you, their representatives, for what you have already done and for what we will do together.

Tonight, we face new and sudden national challenges. We will come together to improve air safety, to dramatically expand the number of air marshals on domestic flights, and take new measures to prevent hijacking. We will come together to promote stability and keep our airlines flying, with direct assistance during this emergency. (Applause.)

We will come together to give law enforcement the additional tools it needs to track down terror here at home. (Applause.) We will come together to strengthen our intelligence capabilities to know the plans of terrorists before they act, and find them before they strike. (Applause.)

We will come together to take active steps that strengthen America's economy, and put our people back to work.

Tonight we welcome two leaders who embody the extraordinary spirit of all New Yorkers: Governor George Pataki, and Mayor Rudolph Giuliani. (Applause.) As a symbol of America's resolve, my administration will work with Congress, and these two leaders, to show the world that we will rebuild New York City. (Applause.)

After all that has just passed — all the lives taken, and all the possibilities and hopes that died with them — it is natural to wonder if America's future is one of fear. Some speak of an age of terror. I know there are struggles ahead, and dangers to face. But this country will define our times, not be defined by them. As long as the United States of America is determined and strong, this will not be an age of terror; this will be an age of liberty, here and across the world. (Applause.)

Great harm has been done to us. We have suffered great loss. And in our grief and anger we have found our mission and our moment. Freedom and fear are at war. The advance of human freedom — the great achievement of our time, and the great hope of every time — now depends on us. Our nation — this generation — will lift a dark threat of violence from our people and our future. We will rally the world to this cause by our efforts, by our courage. We will not tire, we will not falter, and we will not fail. (Applause.)

It is my hope that in the months and years ahead, life will return almost to normal. We'll go back to our lives and routines, and that is good. Even grief recedes with time and grace. But our resolve must not pass. Each of us will remember what happened that day, and to whom it happened. We'll remember the moment the news came — where we were and what we were doing. Some will remember an image of a fire, or a story of rescue. Some will carry memories of a face and a voice gone forever.

And I will carry this: It is the police shield of a man named George Howard, who died at the World Trade Center trying to save others. It was given to me by his mom, Arlene, as a proud memorial to her son. This is my reminder of lives that ended, and a task that does not end. (Applause.)

I will not forget this wound to our country or those who inflicted it. I will not yield; I will not rest; I will not relent in waging this struggle for freedom and security for the American people.

The course of this conflict is not known, yet its outcome is certain. Freedom and fear, justice and cruelty, have always been at war, and we know that God is not neutral between them. (Applause.)

Fellow citizens, we'll meet violence with patient justice — assured of the rightness of our cause, and confident of the victories to come. In all that lies before us, may God grant us wisdom, and may He watch over the United States of America.

Thank you. (Applause.)

MY COUNTRY 'TIS OF THEE

1 My country, 'tis of thee, sweet land of
2 My native country, thee, land of the
3 Let music swell the breeze, and ring from
4 Our fathers' God, to thee, author of

lib-er-ty, of thee I sing; land where my
no-ble free, thy name I love; I love thy
all the trees sweet free-dom's song; let mor-tal
lib-er-ty, to thee we sing; long may our

fa-thers died, land of the pil-grim's pride,
rocks and rills, thy woods and tem-pled hills;
tongues a-wake, let all that breathe par-take,
land be bright with free-dom's ho-ly light;

from ev-ery moun-tain-side let free-dom ring.
my heart with rap-ture thrills like that a-bove.
let rocks their si-lence break, the sound pro-long.
pro-tect us by thy might, great God, our King.

Words: Samuel Francis Smith (1808-1895)
Music: *America*, from *Thesaurus Musicus*, 1745

INDEX